NoSew
Decorating

NoSew Decorating

Fast, Fun & Fusible Craft Projects

Karen E. Kunkel

Sterling Publishing Co., Inc.
New York
A Sterling/Sewing Information Resources Book

Dedication

To Bill and Emilie
For ever
and always

Owner: JoAnn Pugh-Gannon
Photography: Brian Krause, Butterick Studio
Book Design: Rose Sheifer, Graphic Productions, Walnut Creek, California
Illustrations: Elace Comrie, Graphic Design
Index: Anne Leach

All rights reserved.

Library of Congress Cataloging-in-Publication Data
Kunkel, Karen E.
      Fast, fun & fusible : nosew crafting / Karen E. Kunkel.
        p.   cm.
A Sterling/Sewing Information Resources Book

1 3 5 7 9 10 8 6 4 2

First paperback edition published in 1998 by
Sterling Publishing Company, Inc.
387 Park Avenue South, New York, N.Y. 10016
Originally published in hardcover under the title
Fast, Fun & Fusible
© 1997 by Karen E. Kunkel
Distributed in Canada by Sterling Publishing
% Canadian Manda Group, One Atlantic Avenue, Suite 105
Toronto, Ontario, Canada M6K 3E7
Distributed in Great Britain and Europe by Cassell PLC
Wellington House, 125 Strand, London WC2R 0BB, England
Distributed in Australia by Capricorn Link (Australia) Pty Ltd.
P.O. Box 6651, Baulkham Hills, Business Centre, NSW 2153, Australia
Printed in Hong Kong
All rights reserved

Sterling ISBN 0-8069-8645-X

Table of Contents

Introduction

Fantastic Fusibles

Rather press than sew?

Stitchless sewing requires no needles, no thread, just adhesives and a touch of your iron. Fantastic fusibles are all you need to create decorations for your home or beautiful, but simple gift items.

Fusibles are adhesive products that, when ironed between two layers of fabric, turn to glue under heat and adhere the fabrics together. Difficult sewing tasks are accomplished quickly, easily, and with professional results. Use fusibles to seam two layers of fabric, hem a raw edge, bind a cut edge, or apply trim, fringe, or tassels. Create no-sew appliqués, make perfect covered cording, or laminate a fabric.

Adhesives come in many forms. Some can be ironed directly to a project while others have a paper backing that acts as protection between the adhesive and your iron. Paper-backed fusibles allow you to apply the adhesive exactly where desired; then peel away the backing and permanently fuse it to an item.

Other fusible types include fusible fleece batting, liquid fusibles, iron-on tapes, shade backings, fusible trims and lace edgings, fusible waterproof vinyl, and much more. Most are available in different weights (light to super hold) for use with various types of fabric. Some are purchased by-the-yard for application on large sections, while others are packaged in rolls in precut widths (¼", ⅜", ⅝", ¾", ⅞" and 2") for smaller jobs. Tubes of glue, cones of thread, vinyl sheets, ready-to-use patches, hook-and-loop tape and shirring tapes are all ready for fusing.

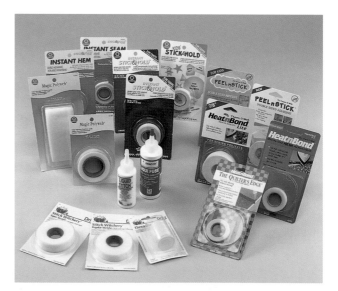

Fantastic Fusibles

Fusible Webbing	Adhesive fibers available by-the-yard or packaged in pre-measured widths.
Fusible Webbing Strips	Adhesive in precut $1/4$" - 2" wide widths.
Fusible Webbing Strips, paper-backed	Adhesive strips with a paper backing in precut $1/4$" - $3/4$" wide widths. Double-stick strips are available for temporary bonding or for a permanent bond after ironing.
Fusible Transfer Web, paper-backed	Adhesive with a transparent paper backing (or release paper), that peels away after ironed to a fabric, then fused where desired. Available by-the-yard.
Fusible Fleece Batting	Polyester batting with adhesive on one side.
Fusible Shade Backing	Nonwoven, stiff backing with one adhesive side. Available by-the-yard or in a prepackaged kit.
Fusible Drapery Tapes	Shirring, pleating, and smocking tapes with rows of adhesive on back side.
Fusible Hook-and-Loop Tape	Adhesive backed loop tape with hook tape (hook portion needs to be glued or stapled).
Fusible Interfacing	Adhesive-backed material (woven and non-woven types) that provides stability and firmness to a fabric.
Fusible Craft Backing	Firm fusible backing adds stiffness and body to fabric for extra support.
Fusible Craft & Pattern Paper	Adhesive-backed paper with $1/4$" grid marks. Temporary bonds to fabric and can be re-ironed. Permanently bonds to tissue paper.
Liquid Fabric Glue	Clear drying fusible type; or, dries on its own for a permanent bond.
Lace & Trim	Adhesive-backed trims in pre-measured lengths are available in various colors.

Note: Always check manufacturer's directions for care. Most fusible products are machine washable, although dry cleaning is not recommend.

Chapter 1

Tools, Tips and Techniques

Before getting started you will need to gather some basic tools and supplies.

Iron

The most integral part of fusing is an iron. A good quality iron will make fusing faster, easier and produce better results. Since many adhesive products call for steam, an iron with good steam capacity is a must. One with a steam controller or burst of steam is helpful. A selection of temperature settings comes in handy for fusing various adhesive weights.

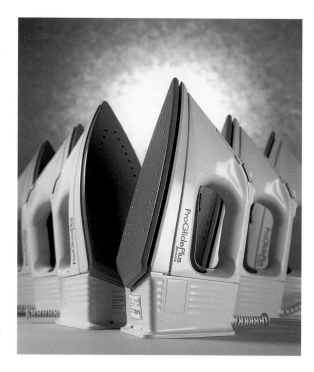

You also may want to consider a steam press for larger fusing jobs. A press looks like a dry cleaner's piece of equipment with its wide flat surface. A press will more uniformly fuse larger areas.

Keeping your iron clean is a challenge when fusing. It is a good idea to have an iron cleaner on hand to remove any residue left from the webbing. Use a piece of paper toweling or a dryer sheet on a warm iron.

Quick Tip

Use baking soda, water and paper towels or a soft cloth to wipe the soleplate of a cool iron to remove adhesive build-up.

Press Cloth

A pressing cloth used between your iron and the fusible fabric helps limit frequent cleanings. Transparent Teflon™ coated sheets (9" x 12" or 11½" x 18") protect your iron and ironing board.

 Brown paper will also serve well as a protective mat and presscloth.

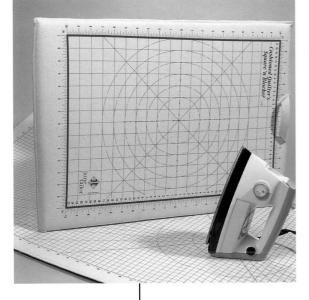

Ironing Surface

A traditional fold-down ironing board is fine for most jobs but a larger pressing surface works best when fusing. To make a do-it-yourself fusing board, pad a plywood board cut to the desired size (36" square or if you have the room, 45" x 60"). Layer cotton batting, until it is about ½" thick, and place an old flannel blanket on top. Then, wrap the entire surface with a heavy cotton fabric or an old sheet. Staple all the edges to the underside of the board. This padded board is great not only for fusing but also as a cutting and pinning surface.

 Use an old hollow door in place of plywood for your padded work surface.

Scissors

A good pair of fabric shears with 8" blades gives a smooth, clean cut for long, straight edges. Cuticle or curved embroidery scissors are helpful for cutting around design motifs. And pinking shears are great for cutting a decorative finished edge before fusing.

Utility knife

A sharp untility knife is perfect for cutting foam-core and mat board.

Fabric Markers

An air-soluble "vanishing" marker disappears within hours while water-soluble markers are removed with the aid of water.

Measuring Aids

Try a transparent ruler, a tape measure, or a carpenter's square when straightening fabric.

Pins

Good quality, long, sharp pins are essential.

Miscellaneous Tools

A staple gun and staples or a hot-glue gun and glue sticks (fabric glue sticks are available for the glue gun) are valuable tools when finishing your projects.

HELPFUL NOTIONS

- Hot Tape™ is a ⅝"-wide adhesive tape designed to withstand heat. Use it to position ribbons, trims and appliques. It is reusable and peels off without leaving a sticky residue on your fabric or iron.

- Quilter's Blocker is a padded surface for pressing and pinning with preprinted grid markings.

- Craft and Pattern Paper is an iron-on paper with ¼" grid marks. It can be fused to fabric temporarily or to tissue paper permanently.

- A glue stick will temporarily hold fabric layers and cardboard together. It works on wood surfaces too.

- Liquid sealant or Fray Check™ is applied to cut ends to prevent raveling.

- A rotary cutter with its rolling blade simplifies cutting long, straight edges. Because it is so sharp, it must be used with a special mat board.

FUSING WITHOUT A FUSS

Fusibles work best when these simple guidelines are followed.

BEFORE PRESSING

1. If possible, pre-wash your fabric for best bonding results.

2. Always work on a clean, smooth, and firm surface.

3. Cut the fusible slightly smaller than the fabric to avoid getting any adhesive on your iron and board.

4. Do a "press test" before fusing on the actual project. Test the adhesive on a scrap of fabric, then jot down the ideal temperature, best fusing time, steam or no steam, and with or without a press cloth.

5. When drawing designs on fusible transfer paper, remember to reverse them since the designs are flipped when fused.

6. If it is difficult to distinguish the adhesive side of fusible fleece, use an air-soluble marker and mark the fusible side. Some manufacturer's indicate the adhesive side with a marking along the edges.

DURING PRESSING

1. To fuse large surfaces, begin at the center and work out.

2. When fusing paper-backed webbing, place the transfer web, paper side up, on the wrong side of the fabric; place iron on paper side and press.

3. When fusing fabrics and fleece to cardboard, press three to five seconds only. More time may cause the cardboard to warp.

4. For a stronger bond, use a damp press cloth when fusing fleece. Place the fleece, fusible side up, on a flat surface; then, place the fabric, right side up, on top of the fleece. Press.

5. When applying adhesive to a corner, fuse along one side and then fuse to the other side, overlapping the ends. Secure any unfused area with liquid fabric glue.

6. Be careful not to over-fuse. When too much heat is applied to some webs, the adhesive will seep through to the right side of the fabric creating an insufficient bond, or no bond at all. Follow the manufacturer's instructions carefully.

AFTER PRESSING

1. After fusing, allow the fabric to cool before handling. Once cool, apply pressure lightly on the right side.

2. After fusing paper-backed transfer web and shade backing, check for air bubbles on the right side of your fabric. Bubbles indicate a poor bond. Press the fabric again on the right side and allow to cool.

3. If you find an area that has not fully bonded, re-apply heat and pressure with your hand on the iron.

4. Do not place warm, fused pieces of fabric on top of one another, or they may stick together.

OOPS!

What happens when a mistake is made? If fabric has been incorrectly fused, simply cover the area with a damp press cloth and press. Gently lift the fabric while it is still warm; then re-fuse.

Liquid glue can be removed with water before it dries.

GENERAL TECHNIQUES

For basic applications use these general techniques, which are referred to throughout this book.

Fuse-Basting

Before permanently fusing two layers of fabric together, place fusible webbing between the layers on the wrong side; then fuse in place.

Fuse Bindings

Fuse transfer web to the inside of purchased double-fold bias bindings, and remove the paper backing. Wrap binding around an edge to encase it, folding under the ends. Fuse in place. Apply liquid fabric glue at the ends.

Quick Tip To make your own self-fabric bias binding strips, cut a bias strip four times the desired finished width; press under each edge to the inside, then press in half lengthwise. Attach to your project in the same manner as purchased binding.

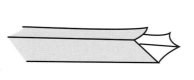

Fuse-Hemming

Press the hem to the wrong side. Place a strip of fusible webbing under the pressed hem and fuse in place.

Double Fused Hem

Press the hem to the wrong side. Fold a second time and press. Place a strip of fusible webbing under the pressed hem close to the cut edge; then fuse in place.

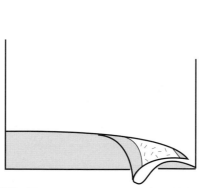

Glue Hemming

Press the hem to the wrong side. Place a bead of liquid fabric glue close to the cut edge. Finger-press the hem and fuse, or allow the glue to dry, following manufacturer's instructions.

Quick Tip

To fuse a narrow hem along a curve, unroll 1' - 2' of a ⅜"-wide fusible webbing strip. Position it even with the bottom edge (right side) of the fabric. Then, fuse on 2' to anchor it; let the strip cool. For the remaining hem, fuse-baste it in place by pressing the fusible strip bottom edge only, allowing the strip's top edge to ease in or "shrink up" as it curves around the edge. Use one hand to guide the strip in place, while holding the iron in the other hand and following with the tip of the iron. When you have the entire section of the strip fuse-basted, lightly press the strip's full width in place by continuing to lift and reposition the iron — do not glide the iron. Hem, turning under the ⅜" strip two times and pressing it in place, while easing in the strip with your lead hand and following with the tip of the iron.

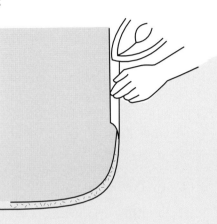

Fuse Openings

Sandwich a fusible webbing strip between open edge, fuse in place.

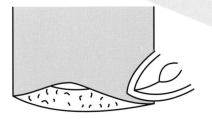

Fuse-Seam

With fabric right sides together, place fusible webbing just inside the seamline (use ½" seams throughout). Fuse the two fabrics together. Allow to cool. Check bonding and iron again, if needed. Press seams to one side.

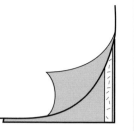

Fuse-Seam for Matching

This technique is useful when matching is required. Place paper-backed fusible transfer web just inside the seamline on the fabric's right side. Fuse according to the manufacturer's directions. Press under the seam allowance on the remaining section. Remove paper backing and lap the pressed edge over the webbing, lining up the seamlines. Fuse and allow to cool. Check bonding; press again if needed.

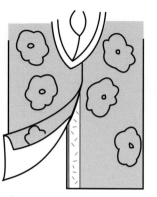

Fuse Trims

Depending upon the width of the trim, cut strips of transfer web, or use precut widths and fuse to the wrong side. Remove paper backing and pin the trim in place. Fuse slowly. Be careful not to overpress or apply excessive pressure, crushing the trim. If a trim cannot be fused, or when applying in a difficult to press area, use liquid fabric glue. Apply glue to the trim and position on the project.

Quick Tip Purchase adhesive-backed trims and lace edgings that have paper-backed webbing in place. They are available in pre-measured lengths.

Mitering Corners

Turn under the cut edge and press. Press the edge again for the desired width. Miter the corner by opening out the pressed edges. At the cross-point, cut the fabric diagonally at the corner to eliminate bulk.

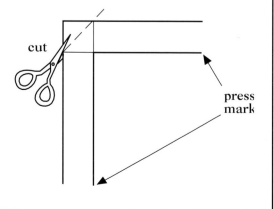

cut

press mark

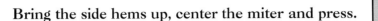

Fold in at the corner at the intersection and press.

Bring the side hems up, center the miter and press.

Sandwich a strip of fusible webbing inside hem and fuse in place.

Mitering Trim Corners

Fuse trim along one side ending at the corner. Fold the trim back up on itself and press. Fold trim diagonally and turn it at a 90° angle.

Fuse in place. Apply a dab of liquid glue under the corner to secure.

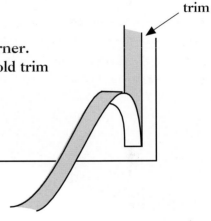

trim

Machine Basting

Use a long machine stitch to temporarily assemble a project. Loosen the machine's needle thread tension and use the longest stitch length setting.

Cutting and Scoring

When cutting mat and foam-core boards use a sharp utility knife to get a clean cut edge. Change the blade often for a good cut. Use a metal ruler as a straight edge to avoid cutting plastic rulers. To score a board, cut through the first layer only and crease along the line, folding away from the scoring.

Straightening Fabric

cut edge

selvage

Before cutting fabric, square one crosswise edge of the fabric. Use a T-square and a marker to draw a line straight across the fabric, from selvage to selvage. Cut on this line.

QUICK TIPS FOR USING FUSIBLE SHIRRING TAPES

Before fusing tapes to fabric, use a pin to pull the cords ½" from the finished edge of the fabric. This will prevent the ends from being fused down. Just before gathering the tape, warm the tape by holding a steam iron just above it. This will make shirring easier.

After the gathering is complete, set the shirring or pleats in place by gently steaming in position. Allow to cool before moving.

FUSIBLE APPLIQUÉS

Some fusible transfer webs have paper backing with grid markings for cutting strips and shapes or pre-printed appliqué designs. Most are tracing paper thin allowing you to trace your own designs directly onto them. Once this paper is fused, it simply releases when pealed away creating a non-raveling edge that can be directly fused onto a surface.

When assembling two or more appliqués with overlapping pieces, use a Teflon™-coated fabric sheet to pre-position the multiple pieces. Iron, let cool, and peel the paper away. You now have one complete appliqué ready to be fused.

HANDY HAND-WORK

Some hand or machine sewing may be required to complete a fusible project.

Hand Basting

Make a long running stitch, weaving the needle in and out of the fabric. Make stitches approximately ¼" long.

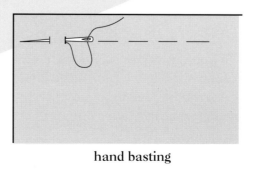

hand basting

Slipstitch

Guide the needle through a folded edge, then pick up a thread from the fabric underneath.

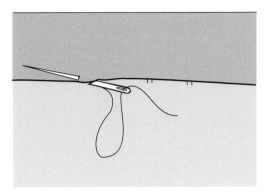

Running Stitch

Make long permanent stitches that weave in and out of the fabric, spaced about $\frac{1}{8}$" apart.

Gathering Stitch

Use a running stitch to draw up fullness. Hand or machine stitch along the seamline then again inside the seamline ($\frac{1}{2}$"). Leave a long thread at both ends of the stitching. Gently pull on one of the threads to gather fabric. Secure thread ends around a straight pin, wrapping in a figure 8, as shown.

anchor thread
around pin

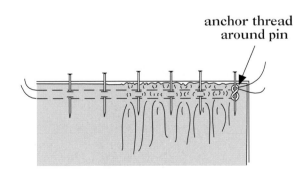

Chapter 2

Kitchen Accents

From windows to table toppers, it all begins with the fabric. Choose one large floral and fruit motif print fabric to set the theme and match it with a check, then add a solid color or two.

Reversible Valance with Ruffle

A reversible valance works double-time in the kitchen.

Materials

- Light- to medium-weight decorator fabric
- Contrasting fabric for lining
- Iron-on shirring tape, twice the width of your window
- Paper-backed, fusible transfer web
- Tension rod

How-to

1. Measure the window width from inside the frame. Measure from the top inside-frame to the window meeting rails (the halfway point of a double-hung window, or to the desired length.) Add 12" for foldover.

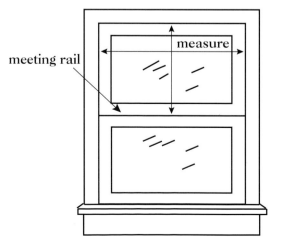

2. Cut the fabric and lining according to your window measurements adding ½" all around. On the lower edge, cut the corners at a slight curve using a plate or other round object as a guide.

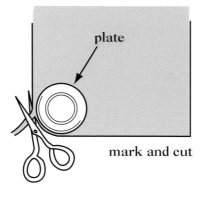

plate

mark and cut

3. Cut a ruffle 7" wide and twice the window width measurement. Cut shirring tape the ruffle length plus 6".

4. Fuse-seam (see General Techniques) the fabric and lining together along three edges of the valance leaving the lower curved edge open. Trim across the corners to eliminate bulk. Press ½" to the wrong side along the open edge. Turn the valance right side out and press.

5. Press ½" to the wrong side along the two short ends of the ruffle, and fuse. With wrong side together, press the ruffle in half lengthwise. Fuse-baste (see General Techniques) the lengthwise edge together. Fuse the short ends together. Fuse shirring tape to this lengthwise fuse-basted edge of the ruffle. Tie the cords together at one end of the tape. Pull the cords at the opposite end so the ruffle measures the finished width of the valance. Cut away any excess tape.

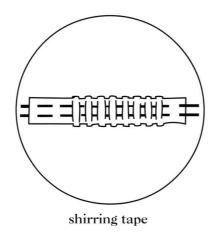

shirring tape

6. Pin the gathered ruffle to the valance at the opening under the pressed edges. Fuse each pressed edge in place over the ruffle.

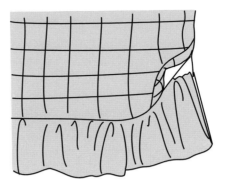

7. To hang, place the tension rod on the top inside-frame of the window. Fold the valance over the rod and adjust the length.

Fringed Placemats

Fringe is fast with just a little sewing and no fusing.

Materials

▮ ¾ yd of loosely woven fabric such as linen or duck. (This will make 4 placemats.)

▮ Optional: needle and thread

How-to

1. Cut placemats 13" x 18". Be sure to cut the fabric on a straight edge (see General Techniques, Straightening Fabric).

2. To fringe the edges, stitch a row of hand or machine running stitches, 1" in from the edge. Using a pin, pull out the threads until the fringe reaches the line of stitching.

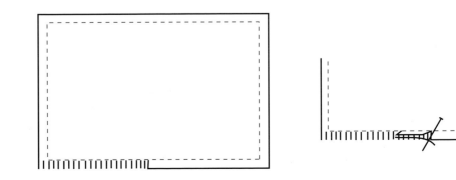

Ribbon Trimmed Napkins

Materials

- 1 yd of light- to medium-weight woven fabric with no distinct right or wrong side. (This will make four 15" x 15" napkins.)
- 6 ½ yds coordinating grosgrain ribbon – ⅜"-wide
- Paper-backed fusible transfer web – ⅜"-wide strips

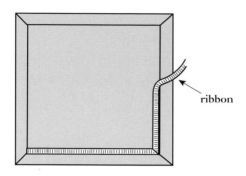

ribbon

How-to

1. Cut 4 napkin squares, 16" x 16".

2. Press ½" to the right side around all the edges. Cut diagonally at the corners and miter (see General Techniques, Mitering Corners).

3. Place the fusible web on the wrong side of the ribbon. Remove the paper backing and fuse in place over cut edges on the napkins.

Border Napkins

Materials

- 1 yd of fabric (This will make 4 – 15" x 15" napkins.)
- ½ yd of contrast fabric for borders
- ½ yd of 36"-wide paper-backed, fusible transfer web
- 2 yds ribbon for napkin rings

How-to

1. Cut 4 napkin squares, 15" x 15". Cut 16 borders out of contrasting fabric, 3" x 15". Cut 16 strips of transfer web, 2" x 15".

2. Press ½" to the wrong side along all edges of napkin and lengthwise edges of border sections.

3. Fuse transfer web over pressed edges of border sections. Allow to cool and remove paper backing. Place bands for border over the pressed edges of the napkin. Trim one end of the band even with the napkin. Miter the overlapping band at the corner by turning under the band at a 45° angle and fusing.

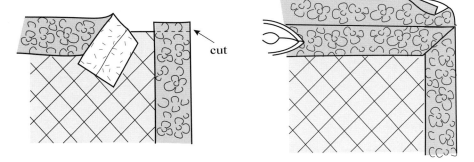

cut

4. Apply glue to any unfused area at the corners.

5. To display, roll the napkin so that the border is shown and tie with ribbon to make a napkin ring.

Quick Tip If you have leftover fabric, make extra napkins to use as basket liners.

Appliqued Hand or Dish Towel

Materials

▌ Purchased hand towel or coordinating fabric – approximately 19" x 27"

▌ Print fabric for appliqué

▌ Paper-backed fusible transfer web

How-to

1. If using coordinating fabric for the hand towel, cut a 19" x 27" rectangle. Fuse a ½" hem around all edges.

2. Select a pattern or design motif that would best suit the towel appliqué. Fuse transfer web to the wrong side of the printed fabric over the motif. Cut away excess fabric around the motif with sharp scissors.

3. Carefully remove the paper backing from the motif and iron into position on the towel using a damp cloth and a hot iron, or follow the manufacturer's instructions.

Appliance Covers

Kitchen essentials like the toaster and coffee maker are not overlooked. Matching appliquéd appliance covers complete the kitchen.

Materials

- Purchased appliance covers
- Printed fabric for appliqués
- Paper-backed fusible transfer web

How-to

1. Select a pattern or design motif that would best suit the appliqué. Fuse transfer web to the wrong side of the printed fabric over the motif. Cut away excess fabric around the motif with sharp scissors.

2. Carefully remove the paper backing from the motif and iron into position on appliance cover using a damp cloth with a hot iron, or follow the manufacturer's instructions.

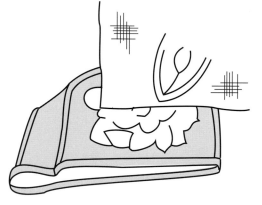

Quick Tip Since appliance covers are odd shapes, it will help to use a rolled up towel to stuff inside the cover when fusing the appliqués in place.

Framed Picture

Can't find just the right piece of artwork for your kitchen wall? Make it yourself with a quick and easy fused-fabric appliqué technique.

Materials

- Cut appliqué motifs from decorator fabric
- ⅜" wide grosgrain ribbon
- Fusible transfer web, lightweight
- ⅜"-wide lightweight, fusible webbing strips
- 16" x 18" frame (or size to suit your appliqué design)
- Coordinating mat board cut to fit frame size
- Transparent ruler
- Pencil

How-to

1. Decide on the motifs you are going to use. Cut the motifs from fabric leaving 1" border all around. Fuse paper-backed transfer web to the motif. Cut the motif from the fabric with sharp scissors.

2. Place the cut motifs on a mat board and arrange as desired.

3. Divide the mat board into equal parts to accommodate the appliqué motifs. The ribbon is used to separate the appliqués. Position a see-through ruler between the appliqué motifs and draw a positioning line for the ribbon. Place the ribbon length on the mat and cut each corner of the ribbon on the diagonal for a mitered finish.

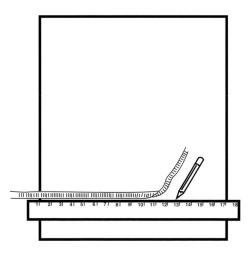

4. To apply the ribbon, use pre-measured strips of fusible web for low-temperature applications. Following the manufacturer's instructions, apply iron-on webbing to the wrong side of the ribbon.

5. After removing the paper, fuse the appliqués and ribbons in place on the mat board with a dry iron and a press cloth.

Quick Tip **Apply seam sealant along the cut end of the ribbon to prevent fraying.**

Tablecloth

Let your tablecloth be the start of an interesting meal.

Materials

- Decorator fabric
- Fusible webbing strips – ½" wide

How-to

1. To determine the finished tablecloth size, measure the length of the tabletop, adding 20" for a 10" drop. Add 1" to this measurement for the hem. Measure the table width, adding 20" for the side drops and 1" for the hem allowance.
   Determine the amount of yardage to purchase by multiplying the number of panels by the cutting length. Convert inches to yards by dividing by 36".

2. After cutting the tablecloth according to the determined measurements, fuse a ½" hem around all cut edges.

Floor Cloth

For fun underfoot, fuse together a customized floor cloth.

Materials

- 2 ¼ yds of 54"-wide heavy-weight fabric such as cotton duck or upholstery fabric (This will make a 4' x 6' finished rug.)
- 2 ¼ yds of 54"-wide fabric for contrasting border

- 4 yds paper-backed fusible transfer web, ultra hold
- Non-skid mat to use under the cloth
- T-square and fabric marker

How-to

1. Straighten the fabric using the T-square and marker (see General Techniques.) Pull a thread at each squared edge and cut along the pulled thread. Cut fabric to 4' x 6'.

2. To make a 4" wide band, cut 2 fabric strips – 10" x 80", and 2 – 10" x 56". (Note: To cut a diagonal border from a contrasting border, find the bias of the fabric by folding at a 90° angle. Press a crease in the fabric along the fold. Measure 10" for band width.)

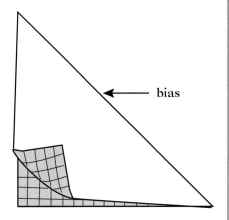

3. Press under ½" along each long edge of the banding strips. Cut the transfer web into 9" wide strips and the length of each band. Fuse the transfer web to each band over the pressed edges. Remove the paper backing and wrap the band around each edge of the floor cloth. Trim one end of the band even with the floor cloth outer edge.

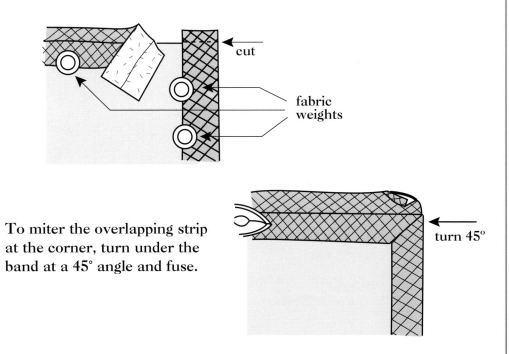

To miter the overlapping strip at the corner, turn under the band at a 45° angle and fuse.

27

Apply glue to any unfused area at the corners. Use a weight on the corners to help bond the layers. Working around the cloth, repeat these steps to apply the remaining band. Turn the floor cloth over and fuse the bands to the underside.

 Hot glue a non-skid mesh rug liner (available in department stores) to the wrong side of the floor cloth to make it slip-proof.

Table Centerpiece

A beautiful topiary tree will accent your table all year round. Use flowers and fruit to coordinate with your fabric. The finished centerpiece measures 26" high.

Materials

- 8" terra-cotta pot
- Block of floral foam
- 4" styrofoam ball
- Artificial pine boughs
- Grape clusters and other artificial fruits
- Silk flowers with leaves
- Dried yarrow in coordinating color
- 3 or 4 – 16" long twigs or branches
- 2 yds of wired ribbon
- Hot-glue gun and glue
- Wire cutters

How-to

1. Insert the floral foam into the pot to fit tightly, and glue. Place the branches into the center of the foam, making sure they are secure. Glue.

2. Carefully push the styrofoam ball onto the top of sticks. Glue in place.

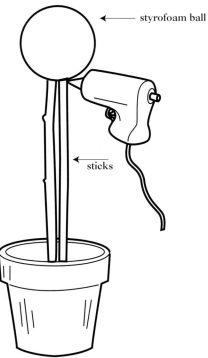

styrofoam ball

sticks

3. Using the wire cutters, cut the pine bough into 3" – 4" pieces. Poke into the ball and foam in base covering the entire surface.

4. Cut apart the fruit, flowers, and leaves; insert into base and tree top in desired locations. Secure with hot glue. Cut yarrow and place on tree with hot glue. Tuck ribbon into tree top to fill any open spaces.

ribbon

Quick Tip Rather than purchasing individual fruits, flowers, and leaves, use wreath picks. Simply cut them apart with wire cutters and arrange on topiary.

Make use of those fabric remnants:

- *Create unique napkin rings with mini terra-cotta pots. Remove the bottom of the pot and glue dried or silk flowers on the side. Slide over the napkin.*

- *Purchase extra hand towels and use them for chair covers. Simply place right sides together; then fuse three sides leaving one short end open. Slide onto chair back. Fold up excess if needed.*

- *Make coordinating pillows for your kitchen chairs using the technique described for the napkins for the top. See Chapter 7, Home Decorating Accents for more pillow ideas and construction tips.*

- *If your room has a hanging light fixture (chandelier type), cover the chain and wire with fabric. Simply measure the length, and multiply by two. Measure loosely around the chain for the width, adding 1" seam allowance. Fuse-seam the long edges, right sides together, turn fabric tube to the right side and slide the casing over the chain.*

Chapter 3

Fast and Fabulous Bedroom Decorating

From basic to beautiful. Create a bedroom that imitates a designer look with coordinating bands, trims and accessories. Projects include trimmed white linens, banded towels, keepsake boxes, a covered lampshade, reversible duvet cover, eyelet dust ruffle and bed skirt, accent pillows, a table topper, waste basket, throw rug and bowed bedroom slippers.

Duvet Cover

A duvet cover is basically a large rectangular cover for a comforter. This cover will instantly change the look of a room. It does require some machine sewing, but the straight edges are fast and simple to do.

Materials

- Tightly-woven, medium-weight decorator fabric for duvet cover front (sheeting can be used)
- Coordinating decorator fabric for duvet cover back (same weight as front) plus 11" x 44" strip for facing
- Decorative cording with lip
- 1 duvet (comforter)
- 44" of fusible hook-and-loop tape
- ½"-wide paper-backed, fusible webbing strips
- Water-soluble marker
- Straight pins

How-to

1. For yardage requirement, measure comforter. Determine how many widths are needed by dividing the comforter width by the fabric width. Multiply the number of widths by the length of the comforter. If you are using the same fabric for the front and back, multiply the number of widths by twice the length to calculate yardage needed.

2. Cut fabric panels the length of your comforter plus 1". If fabric panels are not wide enough, join widths to create the cover front and back panels by fuse-seaming them together using ½" seam allowance. Note: Piece panels together by cutting one panel in half lengthwise and fusing it to each side of the center panel. Cut to required width plus 1" for seam allowance. (Do not join panels on back section yet.)

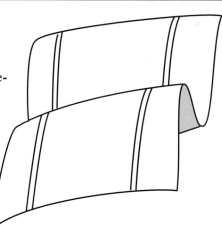

3. Press webbing strip to top side of cording lip, remove paper backing. Fuse cord to the right side of duvet fabric front edges, placing edge of cording to the cut edge of fabric. Ease cording around the corners by slightly rounding them. Cut into the cording lip to ease it around the curved corners.

4. Where the cord ends meet, untwist the cord to separate. Tape each strand end to prevent raveling. Re-twist ends together and glue in place.

5. Cut hook-and-loop tape 44" long.

6. Mark the center of the lower edge of the back section for hook-and-loop placement. Fuse loop tape to the right side of center back panel at the lower seam allowance.

Turn the tape to the wrong side and fuse in place.

7. To make a facing, cut an 11" x 44" strip and press in half lengthwise with wrong sides together. Fuse the cut edges together. Pin hook tape to one side of the facing ½" from cut edge.

8. For duvet back, fuse-seam the side panels to the center back, including the sides of the facing strip. Then, hook center panel and facing sections together.

9. Pin duvet front and back, right sides together, along edges. Machine stitch hook and loop closures, keeping the center of the back panel free.

10. Open hook-and-loop closure and turn duvet cover right side out through the opening. Insert comforter. Close hook-and-loop tape.

 Quick Tip Prevent your comforter from moving inside the duvet cover by stitching ribbons inside each corner of the cover and on the comforter. After inserting comforter into cover, tie ribbons together.

Standard Duvet Sizes	
Twin	66" × 86"
Full/Queen	86" × 86"
King	102" × 86"

Sheets & Pillow Cases

Simple sheets are sensational when fabric bands made from coordinating fabric are added to basic whites.

Materials

- Coordinating fabric to match duvet
- One flat sheet
- Two pillow cases
- Paper-backed fusible transfer web
- ¾"-wide fusible webbing strips

How-to

1. Cut pillow case banding, 9" x 40"; cut trim piece, 2" x 40". Cut sheet banding 9" by the sheet width plus 1"; cut trim 2" by the sheet width plus 1".

2. Fold trim pieces in half lengthwise, wrong sides together, and press. Press ½" along cut lengthwise edge of band. Fuse the trim to the wrong side of the band along the lengthwise pressed edge having 1" of trim extend beyond the band.

3. Press ½" to the wrong side along one short edge of band. Fuse transfer web to banding over pressed edges. Remove paper-backing and iron bands over existing hem on pillow case and sheet header, overlapping ends. Bands will encase entire hem.

Eyelet Dust Ruffle

Designed to cover a box spring mattress, dust ruffles or bed skirts serve to decorate the bed as well.

Materials

- 15"-wide eyelet border fabric or light- to medium-weight fabric

  (Note: With eyelet fabric, there is no hemming involved. Be sure to compare the fabric width to the finished dust ruffle length.) Measure from top of box spring to the floor. To determine yardage, add together three sides of the box spring and double the measurement for fullness (see chart on page 36).

- Velcro™ (hook-and-loop tape) - to fit three sides of the box spring
- Shirring tape
- Pencil-pleat tape or smocking tape that adheres to the hook portion of most brands of hook-and-loop tape to fit three sides of the box spring (see chart on page 36).

Quick Tip **If you are making your dust ruffle of decorator fabric, railroad the fabric by cutting it lengthwise. This will save fabric and often creates an interesting effect when stripes and prints are used.**

How-to

1. If using decorator fabric, cut ruffle sections to equal the box spring length and bottom edge times two for your bed (see chart on page 36), plus 4" for double side hems. Measure width from the top of the box spring to the floor and add 3" for a double hem.

2. Fuse-seam dust ruffle sections together along short ends, with right sides together.

3. Hem one lengthwise edge with a 1" fused double hem. For all fabrics, hem short sides by pressing under 1" double hems on both edges. Fuse in place.

4. Apply the self-adhesive hook tape to the upper side edges and foot edge on the box spring.

hook tape

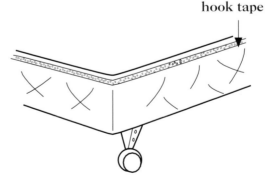

5. Fuse shirring tape so its plush side is face-up on the wrong side of the dust ruffle upper edge. Secure one end of the cording, and pull up on the other end. Then pleat the fabric to the desired finished length and tie off. Attach the dust ruffle to the hook tape on the box spring.

Standard Box Spring Sizes	
Twin	38" × 74"
Full	54" × 74"
Queen	60" × 80"
King	76" × 80"

Bed Skirt

Add a hemmed fabric skirt over the dust ruffle for double impact.

Materials

- Coordinating decorator fabric
- Paper-backed fusible transfer web
- ½"-wide fusible webbing strip

How-to

1. To determine yardage, add 32" to the width measurement of the box spring (12" drop for the two sides and 4" hem allowance) and 16½" to the length measurement. Divide by 36" to determine yards.

2. Cut skirt according to your measurements. Fuse a ½" hem at the upper edge. Cut transfer web into 4" wide strips and fuse to remaining three sides. Remove paper backing and fuse up 4" hems.

3. Place skirt over eyelet dust ruffle adjusting drop so that it is even on the sides and at the end.

Dressing the Bed

• *Use a large bed pillow (50" x 30") to conceal two plain bed pillows for a decorative standout.*
• *Make your bed look more inviting by using a queen size comforter in a double-size duvet.*
• *Fashion two dust ruffles, one of decorator fabric topped by one of lace, for a different take on the bed skirt.*

Table Topper

Purchase a round table cover and personalize it by adding a topper of coordinating fabric. Measurements are given for a 20" diameter round table.

Materials

- 1 yd of 45"-wide light- to medium-weight fabric
- ½ yd coordinating fabric for bands
- Paper-backed fusible transfer web

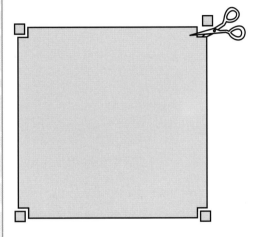

How-to:

1. Cut topper 38" x 38". Cut bands 35" x 5".

2. Press ½" to wrong side along all cut edges of band. Press band in half lengthwise. Cut web into 4" strips measuring 34" long. Fuse along pressed edges of band.

3. Cut a 2" square from each corner of topper.

4. Remove paper-backing form bands and fuse to topper edges, along the extensions. Note that the corners do not overlap.

Banded Waste Basket

Even the trash needs a little dash.

Materials

- 10" tall wicker basket
- Fabric remnants
- 1 yd of ⅜"-wide ribbon for bows
- 1 yd cording without lip
- Iron-on shirring tape
- Paper-backed fusible transfer web
- Hot-glue gun and glue
- Optional: clothes pins

How-to

1. Cut 1 – 6" x 66" strip of fabric and 1 – 4" x 66".

2. Fuse-seam the lengthwise edges of each band. Turn right side out and press so seams are down the center back.

3. Center narrow band over wider band. Hand or machine baste down the center, through all layers. Press under ½" at one short end.

4. Fuse shirring tape to back side of band. Secure cords at one end and pull on the opposite end. Gather band to fit around the upper edge of the basket. Place around basket, securing cords under band. Lap pressed edge over cut edge.

5. Using a hot-glue gun, attach ruffle to upper edge of basket.

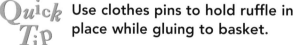 **Use clothes pins to hold ruffle in place while gluing to basket.**

6. Glue the cording to center of band over basting stitches. Cut ribbon into 8" lengths and tie into bows. Glue bows over cording positioning them around the basket.

Covered Lampshade

Spruce up a plain lampshade with decorator fabric for a custom look. Fabric is fused directly to the shade.

Materials

- Lamp and shade
- Fabric – yardage depends on size of shade (make shade pattern first, then measure for fabric requirement)
- Cording without lip
- Paper-backed fusible transfer web
- Liquid fabric glue
- Clothes pins

How-to

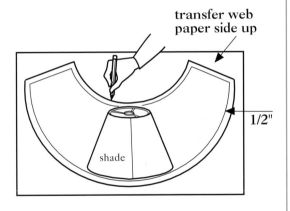

transfer web
paper side up

1/2"

shade

1. Make a pattern for your shade using transfer web. Place the shade on the paper side of the web. Beginning and ending at the seam, roll the shade while you trace the upper and lower edges; add ½" on all edges. Cut transfer web slightly larger than tracing.

2. Iron transfer web to fabric. Allow to cool and cut along outer markings.

3. Center fabric on shade having ½" allowance hang over the edges. Hold in place with clothes pins. Using your iron, fuse in place carefully avoiding wrinkles and bubbles, and overlap the ends. Turn ½" to the inside and fuse using the tip of your iron. Apply liquid fabric glue along seam where short ends meet.

4. Finish the shade by gluing cording at the upper and lower edges.

Quick Tip Glue ends of cording in place, and allow to dry before cutting to avoid excess raveling.

Slippers

Cozy toes need not be forgotten. Embellish a pair of terry scuffs with an artificial flower, doily, or a big bow.

Materials

- Purchased slippers
- Fabric remnant
- ½"-wide fusible webbing strips
- Needle and thread

How-to

1. Cut bow 4" x 24".

2. Press ½" to the wrong side along lengthwise edges. Press in half lengthwise. Fuse pressed edges together. Fuse open ends closed.

3. Tie into a bow and cut ends in an inverted "V".

4. Hand-stitch bows at top of slippers.

Envelope Pillow

Materials

- 1 standard-size pillowcase
- Decorative fabric remnant
- Paper-backed fusible transfer web
- ½"-wide fusible webbing strips
- Covered button kit
- 1 yd cording with a lip
- Rectangular pillow form
- 20" fusible hook-and-loop tape
- Needle and thread
- Water-soluble marker
- Ruler

How-to

1. Measure 12" up from lower edge of pillowcase and mark a line parallel to the edge. Cut the top layer of the case down the center back to the line and cut along the marking to the sides.

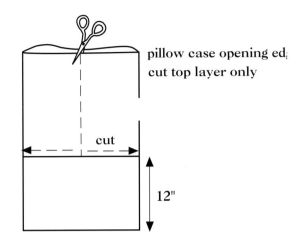

pillow case opening ed;
cut top layer only

cut

12"

2. To form the envelope flap, measure 22" from the lower edge on the front and mark center. Using a ruler, mark a line from the center marking to the sides to form a triangle.

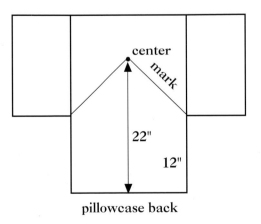

center

mark

22"

12"

pillowcase back

3. Cut decorative fabric ½" larger than triangle.

4. Press under ½" along straight edge of pillowcase and fuse-hem.

5. Cut triangle of fabric 22"-wide and 15" on each side to form the point. Press under ½" along straight edge of triangle. Fuse transfer web to wrong side over pressed edge of triangle section. Allow to cool and remove paper backing. Flip pillowcase so the back is face down on a flat surface. Place fabric triangle over pillow flap turning ½" to the inside along the pointed ends.

6. Using fusible strips, iron cording to the inside edge of pillow flap. Apply liquid glue at ends to secure cord.

7. Cover button with contrasting decorator fabric following manufacturer's instructions. Hand stitch to front of flap at the point.

8. Insert pillow form through opening. Fuse hook-and-loop tape at opening edges to close.

Rosette Neckroll Pillow

Materials

- 1¼ yds of 54"-wide decorator fabric
- 2 yds cording without lip
- 2 tassels
- ½"-wide fusible webbing strips
- 18" x 40" piece of polyester fiberfill batting
- Liquid fabric glue
- 2 rubber bands

How-to

1. Straighten fabric (see General Techniques). Cut a 45" square.

2. Press 8" to wrong side along two opposite ends. Fuse.

3. Place fabric right side down on flat surface. Center batting on wrong side of fabric having edge of fleece even with one cut edge of fabric. Wrap remaining cut end over the batting.

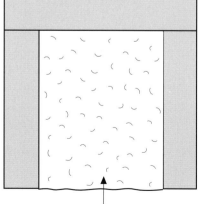

batting

4. Begin rolling the fabric from the cut edge, wrapping the batting. Keep fabric smooth, being careful not to roll too tightly and crush the loft of the batting.

5. Wrap rubber bands tightly around each end that extends beyond the batting to form rosettes. Wrap cording (or ribbon) over rubber band, tucking ends under. Arrange rosettes at each end.

6. With liquid glue, secure lengthwise edge of pillow in place. Allow to dry.

7. Glue cording to pillow front in a decorative pattern for added detail.

Quick Tip Before rolling batting, sprinkle potpourri on fleece. Roll it up for a sweet-smelling neckroll pillow.

Covered Band Boxes

Custom band boxes are used for decoration and storage.

Materials

- Cardboard or papier-mache band box
- Fabric and lining pieces the size of your bandbox (⅝ yard for an 8" x 5" box; ¾ yard for a 10" x 6" or 12" x 7" box)
- Ribbon and trims, as desired
- Paper-backed fusible transfer web
- White craft glue or liquid fabric glue
- Hot-glue gun and glue

How-to

1. Trace around the bottom, side, lid, and lid side pieces of box on paper-backed side of fusible web. Mark a second line ½" outside the first line (do not add ½" to the bottom piece). Fuse paper-backed adhesive to fabric and cut along the second line.

2. For the box inside, trace around the bottom, side, lid and lid side on the paper-backed side of the adhesive. Fuse transfer web to lining fabric and cut on the marked line.

3. Cover the outside of the box with decorator fabric, centering the corresponding piece right-side-up.

4. Fold under one short end and overlap the cut edge. Turn ½" of fabric to inside. Clip lower edge of fabric ¼" and fuse to bottom of box. Fuse, pressing carefully to eliminate wrinkles. For the circles (box lid), clip the seam allowance to within ⅛" of the box. Cover the top then the side separate.

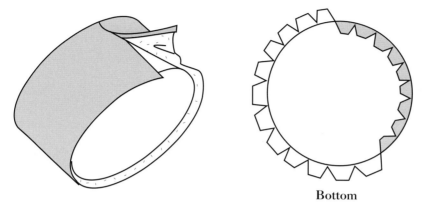

Bottom

5. For the inside, begin by cutting a bottom circle. Using glue, spread on the wrong side of the fabric circle and press into place. Center the corresponding lining piece on the inside covering all cut edges. Fuse.

6. Embellish the outside with ribbon, lace, silk flowers, or bows. Add trinkets, buttons, and beads as desired.

Quick Tip To determine fabric amount, measure the circumference of box and add ½". Determine width by measuring the height of box plus ½".

Trinket Boxes

These catch-all's are fun and easy to do.

Shirred Square Box

Materials

- 15" x 15" piece of cardboard
- ½ yd decorator fabric

Use wooden Shaker boxes and paint the inside using acrylic paint and a sponge brush for a fast finish. Shoe boxes or any cardboard box can be covered with decorator fabric and embellished.

- 4" square of fusible polyester batting
- Paper-backed fusible transfer web
- ⅜"-wide fusible webbing strips
- ½" yd of 1½"-wide grosgrain ribbon
- Liquid fabric glue
- Hot-glue gun and glue

How-to

1. From cardboard, cut 2" x 16" rectangle; 4" square for base; 3¾" square for inner base; and 4¼" square for lid.

2. From fabric, cut 4½" x 32" for shirring strip; 4 - 5" squares for lid, base, and insides. Cut 4" square from batting.

3. Mark a line on cardboard rectangle every 4". Score using a scissors or mat knife along marking so that it will bend. This will be the outside of the box.

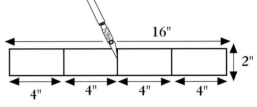

4. To make shirring strip, fold fabric in half lengthwise, right sides together; then fuse cut ends using webbing strips. Turn right side out.

5. Insert cardboard strip into the fabric shirring strip. Slide the fabric along the cardboard, adjusting gathers. Staple the cardboard ends together.

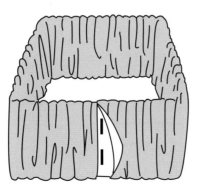

Bend strip at 90° angles where it was scored to form a square. This will be the outside. Fold under one of the fabric ends and glue together.

6. Fuse transfer web to base and inner base fabric squares. Remove paper backing and center cardboard pieces on fabric. Fuse fabric to cardboard wrapping the ends around to the underside.

7. Run a bead of hot glue all around the edge of the underside of the trinket base (the fabric-covered side is the base bottom); then place the shirred square in position. You may need to hold it in place until the glue sets.

Use masking tape to hold the sides in place to the bottom of the box while the glue is drying.

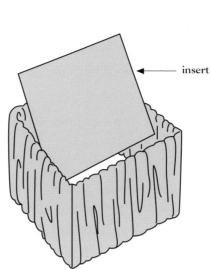

insert

8. Insert inner base, wrong side down, into box. Glue to secure in place.

9. Make trinket box top by fusing batting to lid section. Fuse transfer web to the lid fabric. Remove paper backing and fuse over batting wrapping ends under and fusing in place. Wrap ribbon around center of lid and tie into a bow.

10. Press under ¼" along edges of remaining fabric square and fuse transfer web over pressed edges. Finish by fusing fabric to the underside of the lid covering cut edges and ribbon. Place on box.

Rectangle Trinket Box

Materials

- 22" x 22" piece of cardboard
- ½ yd decorator fabric
- Fusible polyester batting
- Paper-backed fusible transfer web
- ⅜"-wide fusible webbing strips
- Liquid fabric glue
- Hot-glue gun and glue

How-to

1. From cardboard, cut 1 – 2" x 22" for sides; 1 – 8" x 8" square for outside; 1 – 3½" x 8½" for lid; and 1 – 2¾" x 11" for dividers.

2. Cut fabric: 1 – 7" x 23" for sides; 1 – 9" x 9" for base; 1 – 8" x 8" for inside base; 1 – 4½" x 9½" for lid; and 1 – 5" x 12" for dividers. Cut 1 piece of batting, 4½" x 9½".

3. Fuse transfer web to all fabric pieces.

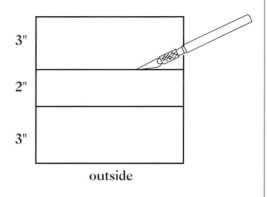

4. For outside, measure 3" from one end, then 2"; mark and score with a scissors or mat knife. Bend along score lines and fuse fabric to cardboard, wrapping cut ends under and mitering corners. (Caution: Do not pull fabric too taut when fusing. Be sure it will bend along score lines. The score lines will be on the outside.) Fuse inside base with fabric, covering cut edges.

outside

5. Measure and mark lines on cardboard side section 8" from one end, then 3"; then 8".

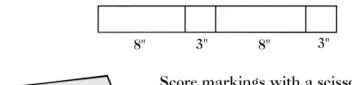

8"   3"   8"   3"

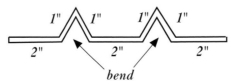

Score markings with a scissors or mat knife. Bend cardboard along score marks to form a rectangle. Cover sides with fabric, having straight edges even with cardboard edge. Glue short ends together at the corner. To form box, glue rectangle to one end of outside section.

6. To make dividers, score cardboard 2" from one end, 1", 1", 2", 1" and 1" as shown. Bend along score lines.

1" 1"   1" 1"

2"   2"   2"

bend

Fuse fabric to cardboard. Insert dividers into box and glue to secure.

7. Fuse batting to cardboard lid section. Fuse fabric over batting wrapping cut ends to the underside. Glue top to outside cover.

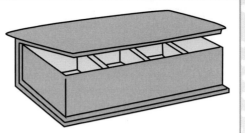

Embellished Bath Towels

Materials

- Purchased bath and hand towels
- Decorator fabric – two different coordinating prints
- 2 yds cording with a lip
- Paper-backed fusible transfer web, ultra hold
- ½"-wide paper-backed fusible webbing strips
- Liquid fabric glue

How-to

1. Cut fabric 6" x 29" (or the width of your bath towel plus 1"); cut coordinating fabric 4" x 29" (or the width of your hand towel plus 1") for the bands.

2. Press ½" to wrong side of all cut edges on fabric bands.

3. Fuse webbing strip to right side of cording lip. Apply liquid fabric glue to ends of cord to prevent raveling. Remove paper-backing on cording and fuse to one long pressed edge of narrow band, turning under at each end.

4. Fuse transfer web to wrong side of bands. Allow to cool and remove backing. Center narrow band with cording on right side of wider band and fuse.

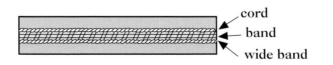

cord
band
wide band

5. Place band on lower edge of towel having ends even; fuse in place.

Fabric Trimmed Accent Rug

Materials

- 29" x 48" rug
- Decorator fabric for trim
- 3 yds of cording without a lip
- Paper-backed fusible transfer web
- Fusible webbing strips, ½"-wide
- Straight pins
- Ruler
- Hot-glue gun and glue

How-to

1. Cut 2 – 5" x 26" and 2 – 5" x 39" trim pieces. Press ½" to wrong side along lengthwise edges.

2. Fuse transfer web over pressed edges of trim pieces. Allow to cool.

3. Place rug on a flat surface. Using a ruler, measure 2" in from each edge and pin-mark.

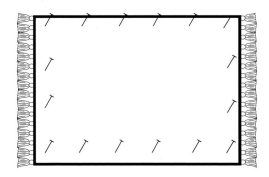

4. Remove paper backing from trim sections and place outer long edge at pin markings. Miter corners of trim (see General Techniques).

5. Hot glue cord to inside edges of trim.

Quick Tip **Consider using sheets for some of the bedroom projects in place of decorator fabric.**

Chapter 4

Bathrooms Plus

Transform a functional bath into one that makes a splash. Purple and yellow floral print shower and window curtains with matching gingham accessories give the bath a fresh look. Smart time- saving fusing techniques are all you need.

Shower Power

Cover your bath with a pretty watercolor print shower curtain. Hang it on the rod by wrapping coordinating ribbon through grommets and around the rod. Finished size 72" x 72" to match a standard shower curtain liner.

Materials

- 5 yds of 45"-wide fabric (allow ½" yard extra to match prints)
- 2 yds of paper-backed fusible transfer web
- ½" x 2"-wide fusible webbing strips
- Plastic shower curtain liner
- ⅜"-diameter grommets equal to number on shower curtain liner
- Grommet pliers
- 10 yds coordinating ribbon
- Air-soluble marker
- Needle and thread
- Scissors
- Hot-glue gun and glue

Quick Tip Use wire ribbon for crisp-looking bows.

How-to

1. Cut 2 panels of fabric 82" long.

2. Fuse-seam the panels together to create a 76" wide panel. Fuse-hem the lower edge with a 3" wide double hem. Fuse-hem the side edges with a 1" double hem (see General Techniques).

3. Fuse a 2" wide strip of fusible web to the wrong side of the curtain's upper edge. Then fuse a 2" deep hem. Press under 2" again and fuse in place close to pressed edge.

4. Using the shower curtain liner as a guide, mark grommet placements at the curtain's upper edge. At each mark, cut holes using a sharp pointed scissors. Attach grommets according to manufacturer's directions.

5. To hang curtain and liner, tack one end of ribbon above first grommet. Loop over rod and pull back through the same grommet. Lace ribbon through remaining holes of curtain and liner, wrapping around shower curtain rod. Pull ribbon so curtain is just below the rod.

6. Hot glue a bow at the end.

Quick Tip Use fabric leftovers to make a matching shower curtain tieback.

Window Valance

Bows tie together a coordinated look on the window.

Materials

- Light- to medium-weight decorator fabric
- Coordinating fabric for trim, tabs, and lining
- 3½ yds of 1½"-wide ribbon
- Fusible webbing strips
- Straight pins

How-to

1. Measure window width from outside of molding. Multiple width measurement by 2.

2. Cut valance 10" by your width measurement. Cut lining 13" by your width measurement. Cut tabs 5" x 7" (Cut a total of 8 tabs for a 48" wide window, depending on your window width.)

3. Fuse-seam valance and lining pieces together to equal your window width measurement.

4. Fold tab pieces lengthwise, right sides together and fuse-seam. Turn right side out and press flat. Fold tabs in half crosswise and place $\frac{3}{4}$" from the ends of the valance, having the cut ends even. Pin in place. Pin remaining tabs to valance, spacing them evenly apart.

To secure tabs, hand or machine stitch $\frac{1}{2}$" from edge. Flip tabs up and press seam allowance down.

5. Press $\frac{1}{2}$" to wrong sides along both long edges of lining. With wrong sides together, pin valance and lining together, having pressed edges even at top (tabs will be poking out the top between the layers). The lower edge of the lining will be 2" longer than the valance. Press $\frac{1}{2}$" to wrong side along short ends of valance and lining. Bring lining to the front and press. Fuse valance and lining together along each of the four sides.

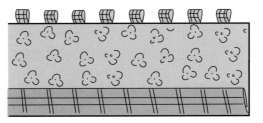

6. Cut ribbon into 16" lengths and tie each into a bow. Hand sew or glue bows to the bottom of each tab.

7. Hang valance on a dowel. Adjust so fullness is evenly distributed.

Tissue Box Cover

A tissue box is dressed for display. This cover fits a 9½" x 4¾" x 1⅞" dispenser-size tissue box, but you can easily adapt the dimensions to fit the box size of your choice.

Materials

- ▌ 2 – 19" x 16" rectangles of decorator fabric (use contrasting fabric for lining, if desired)
- ▌ 2½ yds of 1"-wide coordinating ribbon,
- ▌ Paper-backed fusible transfer web
- ▌ Ruler and pencil

How-to

1. Mark cutting lines on paper side of transfer web measuring 20" x 17". Cut 5½" squares from each corner.

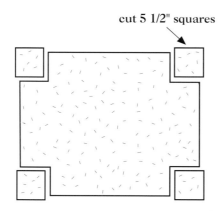

cut 5 1/2" squares

2. Fuse transfer web to fabric and cut along markings. Using this section as a pattern, trace onto remaining fabric and cut.

3. Cut ½" from all edges of paper-backed fabric section. Press ½" to wrong side along edges of remaining section, clipping into the corners.

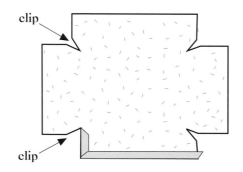

clip

clip

4. Place fabric sections wrong sides together and fuse.

5. Place cover on a flat surface and center tissue box. Bring end flaps and sides up over the box and tie ribbons around ends to secure. Pull tissues through the cover opening.

Custom Mirror Frame

Presiding over the sink is a custom covered mirror.

Materials

- 18" plywood square
- 24" square of decorator fabric
- ½ yd fusible fleece batting
- Paper-backed fusible transfer web
- 2 yds cording with a lip
- 1 yd braid trim
- 16" round mirror
- Hot-glue gun and glue
- Picture hanger
- Jigsaw

How-to

1. Trace a 12" diameter circle from the center of the plywood square. Using a jigsaw, cut along marking to make frame.

2. Place fleece, glue side down on top of frame. For a more padded look, cut two layers of fleece and apply the second directly on top of the first. Cut away fleece along the inside circle of the frame. Lightly fuse fleece to frame.

3. Place transfer web on wrong side of fabric and fuse. Let cool; then remove paper-backing.

4. Center fabric on fleece side of frame. Lightly fuse fabric to fleece. Cut across corners to reduce bulk. Beginning on one side, gently pull the fabric over the edge to the underside of the frame and fuse. Then, turn the frame and fuse the opposite side. Do the same for remaining two sides.

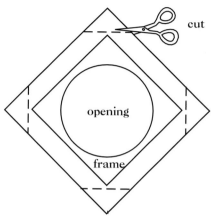

5. Cut away fabric from the inside circle leaving 1" of fabric to turn under. Clip into the curves, being careful not to clip to the edge of the frame. Pull the clipped edges to the frame's wrong side and fuse them into place as you go. Once all the edges are fused, press entire area lightly on both sides and let cool.

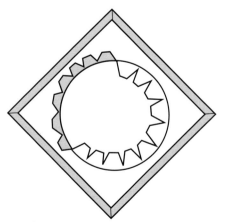

6. Using hot glue, outline the inside frame opening edge with the flat braid trim. Place the cording around the outer edges, gluing lip of cord to back of frame.

7. To hang, attach the picture hanger at the upper edge of one corner and hang with the point up, making a diamond shape.

Cover the frame with velvet and hang in the living room or bedroom for an elegant looking-glass.

Clothes Hamper

Materials

- Purchased clothes hamper
- 2 yds decorator fabric
- 5 yds flat braid trim
- Paper-backed fusible transfer web
- Straight pins
- Fabric marker
- Hot-glue gun and glue
- Screwdriver

How-to

1. Cut fabric to fit hamper sides adding ½" for seam allowances on all edges. If needed, fuse-seam fabric together (see General Techniques).

2. Remove lid from hamper.

3. Press ½" to wrong side along the lengthwise edges and one short end of the fabric. Beginning at the center back, wrap fabric around hamper having pressed edges even with the upper and lower edges of the hamper. Use straight pins to hold fabric in place. Lap pressed edge over cut edge at the center back. Hot glue fabric in place. Hot glue trim to hamper at the upper and lower edges.

4. To cover lid, measure lid and add 4" to the length and width. Measure inside lid and cut lid lining fabric 1" smaller. Fuse transfer web to wrong side of fabric. Remove paper-backing and center lid on wrong side of fabric. Fuse lightly in place on top side. Pull the corners around to the inside lid and fuse.

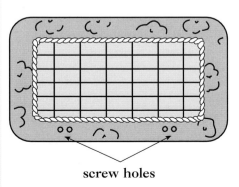

screw holes

5. With a fabric marker, mark location of screw holes.

6. Remove backing from lid lining and fuse over cut edges on inside of lid. Hot glue trim around the edges of lining fabric to finish.

7. Re-attach lid to hamper.

Storage Smarts - Fabric Covered Shelf

Keep bathroom sundries neat and accessible with a utilitarian shelf custom-covered in matching fabric.

Materials

- 5 pieces of ½" thick plywood, 4 pieces – 20" x 4", or 1 piece – 19" x 4" purchased shelves

- 21" x 20" cardboard for shelf back

- Decorator fabric (use contrasting fabric for the back, if desired)

- Paper-backed fusible transfer web

- Drill and screws

- Liquid fabric glue

- Sponge brush

- 2 picture hangers

How-to

1. Cut 5 – 20" plywood pieces. Assemble shelf.

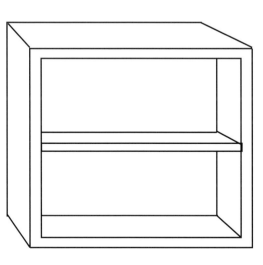

2. Cut fabric for top, sides, bottom and inside of shelf 1" larger than actual shelf measurements. Fuse transfer web to fabric, and remove paper backing. Working in sections, beginning at the top, center fabric over the shelf. Using your iron, fuse fabric in place. Clip into the corners to help the fabric fold under and around the edges.

3. Dilute liquid fabric glue with water. Using a sponge brush, apply a thin coat along the edges to seal.

4. Cut fabric for shelf back ½" larger around all edges than cardboard. Fuse web to wrong side. Cover cardboard, fusing fabric in place. To finish, hot glue cardboard to back of shelf with the fabric right side facing the inside of the shelf and the wrong side to the back.

5. Attach picture hangers to back of shelf at the upper corners. Hang.

Trimmed Towels

Inexpensive towels get sophisticated with the addition of coordinating fabric bands and ribbons to match. Your guests will enjoy the custon coordinated look of your bath when even the towels match.

Materials

- Purchased bath and hand towels
- Decorator fabric
- 2 yds of 1"-wide ribbon
- Paper-backed fusible transfer web, ultra hold
- ⅜"-wide paper-backed fusible webbing strips
- Liquid fabric glue

How-to

1. Cut fabric band 6" x 29" (or the width of your towel plus 1").

2. Press ½" to wrond side along lengthwise edges of fabric band.

3. Cut ribbon 29" long. Fuse webbing strip close to one long edge of ribbon. Apply liquid fabric glue to ends to prevent raveling. Remove paper-backing and fuse ribbon to right side of each long edge of fabric band, having ½" extend along each lengthwise edge. Turn ribbon ends to the wrong side.

ribbon — band — ribbon

4. Cut transfer web 6" x 28". Fuse transfer web to wrong side of band over pressed edges and ribbon. Allow to cool and remove backing. Place band on lower edge of towel, centering band over the woven design on the towel; fuse in place.

Making a Picture Bow

This bow is made in three separate sections for picture perfect results.

Materials

- Decorator fabric
- ½"-wide fusible webbing strips
- Liquid fabric glue
- Small curtain ring
- Needle and thread

How-to

1. For an 8" x 10" frame, cut bow loops 16" x 6"; cut tails 40" x 6"; cut knot 4" x 5".

2. Fuse-seam each loop strip along the lengthwise edge. Turn to the right side and press seam to the lower edge. Bring the ends together to form a loop; then slipstitch or fuse together.

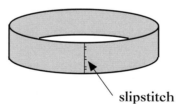

slipstitch

3. Fold the loop at the center and pleat. Fuse-seam the long edges of the knot, right sides together, and turn. Center the knot over the pleat at the loop center and wrap tightly so the loops form a bow. Fuse or hand stitch the knot ends together.

4. Make the tails by fuse-seaming the lengthwise edges right sides together. Turn and press. Fuse the short ends closed. Fold the tail in half lengthwise at a slight angle so the tail flairs out; pin. Glue the tails to the back of the knot. Cut the tails in an inverted "V".

5. To hang bow, hand sew ring to back of knot at center of the bow. Hang bow in position on a picture hook, just above the picture frame.

 Create your own wired fabric bow by using paper-backed webbing on wrong side of loop and placing 24 to 28 gauge beading wire inside the fabric loop along each fold. Fuse in place.

wire

Chapter 5

The Desk Set

Organize your home office with coordinated desk accessories. These hard-working accessories are as attractive as they are useful. Keeping track of shopping lists, correspondence, bills, and family schedules becomes easy and elegant.

Decorator Tissue Box Cover

Decorative touches make an office pretty and practical.

Materials

- ½ yd decorator fabric
- 20" x 30" foam-core board
- ¼ yd fusible fleece
- Paper-backed fusible transfer web
- 27" of cording with tassels
- Hot-glue gun and glue
- Retractable-blade utility knife
- Masking tape
- Ruler
- Pencil

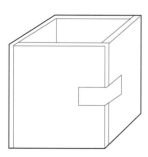

How-to

1. To make box cover, use a ruler and pencil to mark four sides on foam-core board, 5" x 5½" and one 5" square for the top. Using the utility knife and ruler cut along the markings. Glue the four sides together at the long edges. Tape the sides and allow glue to dry.

2. Cut fabric 22" x 8" for the sides. Cut a 6" square of fabric and fleece for the top. Cut 1 piece of fleece 22" x 5½" for the sides.

3. Fuse transfer web to the wrong side of the fabric.

4. Place fleece, fusible side down, on foam-core box. Fuse, butting ends together along the center on one side of the box. Trim fleece even with box top and bottom edges.
   Remove paper backing from the fabric. Beginning at center of one side, place wrong side of fabric over fleece having about 1" extend at the upper and lower ends. Fuse in place, turning ½" to wrong side to finish the end at the center along one side. Wrap fabric over the box at the upper and lower edges and bring the fabric edges to the inside. Fuse in place.

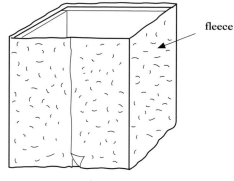

fleece

5. To make box top, cut an opening on the top piece of foam-core board at the center, using a utility knife. Glue batting to top. Fuse fabric over batting. Cut an opening in the fabric and batting, allowing ½" extra fabric for turning under. Slash around the top opening, being careful not to cut beyond the opening.

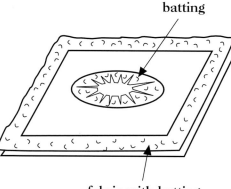

batting

fabric with batting

Tuck fabric around the opening. Turn fabric under at the outer edges mitering the corners. Glue top to box at one end and allow to dry. Tie cording around cover at the box upper edge. Slide the cover over a tissue box.

Telephone Book Cover

Disguise a telephone book with a custom cover.

Materials

- ⅜ yd decorator fabric
- ⅜"-wide paper-backed fusible webbing strips
- Fusible interfacing
- Needle and thread

How-to

1. Cut fabric and interfacing 30" x 12". Fuse interfacing to wrong side of fabric.

2. Fuse webbing strip to wrong side of fabric cover along each short end.

3. Remove paper backing from strip and turn fabric under ⅜" on each end. Fuse in place.

4. On outside of cover, fuse 4½" strips of webbing to the side flaps along the upper and lower edges. Turn flaps to outside and fuse edges right sides together.

webbing strip

5. Turn flaps to the inside and press.

6. To hem upper and lower edges, open out and fuse adhesive strip along inside edges. Remove paper backing and turn hem to inside. Fuse.

7. Before inserting book, secure hem to flap with bar tacks at the upper and lower edges. To bar tack, thread a hand sewing needle and knot end. Insert needle from the inside of the flap and sew four or five stitches through all layers of fabric. Knot thread and trim.

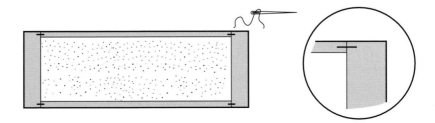

Expandable Folder

A place for everything and everything in its place! Organize your important papers in this handy folder.

Materials

- 1 expandable folder
- ½ yd decorator fabric
- Fusible fleece
- Paper-backed fusible transfer web
- Mat board to fit front and back of folder
- 27" of cording with tassels
- Hot-glue gun and glue

How-to

1. Remove flap by cutting across the upper edge of the file. Measure width and height of folder (when closed) and cut two from mat board. Cut one from fleece. Cut two from fabric adding 1" extra along each edge.

2. Fuse transfer web to wrong side of fabric.

3. For file back, center mat board on wrong side of fabric. Cut across corners to eliminate bulk. Fuse to mat board, mitering corners on wrong side.

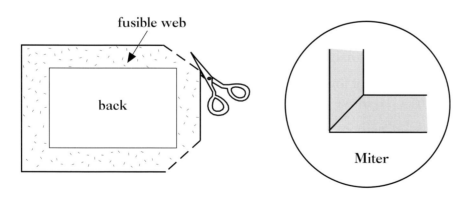

fusible web

back

Miter

4. For front, fuse fleece to remaining mat board section. With fleece side down, center mat board over wrong side of fabric. Fuse in the same way as the back.

5. Cut cording in half. Glue cut end on wrong side of file front and back at the center.

6. To finish, glue the padded front and back covers to the file centering over the folder.

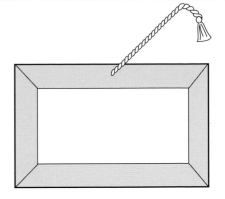

Bulletin Board

Invitations, photos, and notes are handy when placed on this made-to-order bulletin board.

Materials

- Decorator fabric
- Paper-backed fusible transfer web
- Ceiling tile cut to 18" x 24"
- 4 yds flat braid
- ¼ yd braid with tassles
- 27" of twisted cording with tassels
- Flat head tacks or push pins
- Hot-glue gun and glue

How-to:

1. Cut 1 – 22" x 28" piece of fabric for the front; cut 1 – 16" x 22" piece of fabric for the back.

2. Fuse transfer web to wrong side of the fabric sections.

3. For front, place ceiling tile smooth side down on wrong side of fused fabric. Trim fabric diagonally at corners and fuse to tile, wrapping ends to the back and mitering corners (see General Techniques).

4. Remove paper backing and center the back fabric section to the wrong side of the tile, covering all cut edges. Fuse in place.

5. Cut lengths of trim to run diagonally across the board front allowing 2" extra at each end. Pull taut across board on opposite diagonals, keeping lines parallel. Bring ends to the back and glue with hot-glue gun.

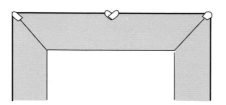

6. Cut small tassels from trim and glue to flat head tacks. Insert tacks at cross points to secure trim

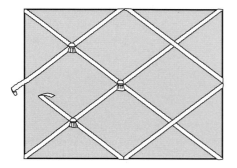 

7. Cut cording with tassles in half and glue each end to back of board about 5" in from the side. Tie ends together and hang.

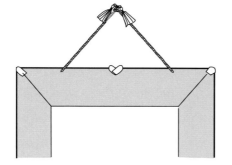

Glue buttons, small silk flowers, or bows to the flat tacks to secure trim on bulletin board.

Note Pad Cover

Materials

- 8" x 20" decorator fabric remnant
- ¼ yd flat braid trim
- 4½" x 14" foam-core board
- Paper-backed fusible transfer web
- Liquid fabric glue
- Pencil and ruler
- Mat knife
- 4" x 6" note paper

How-to

1. Using a mat knife, cut foam-core 4¼" x 14". Measure 6½" from each short end and mark. Using a mat knife or scissors, lightly score along markings being careful not to cut all the way through foam-core.

2. Cut one fleece to match foam-core board. Cut fabric cover 8" x 18" for outside. Cut fabric 4" x 13½" for inside lining.

3. Fuse fleece to scored side of board. To create cover, fold up along scoring.

4. Fuse web to outside fabric and remove paper backing. Place foam-core on flat surface, fleece side up. Center fabric on cover and fuse lightly. Beginning at short ends, fold fabric around board and cut diagonally across corners to eliminate bulk. Fuse in place. Fold side edges up over cover clipping into the fabric at the score marks; fuse.

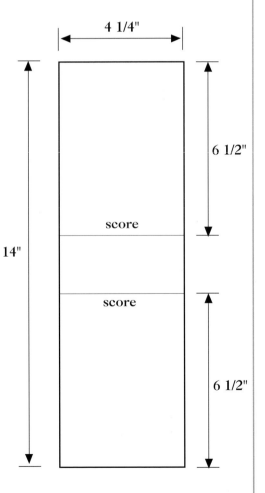

5. Cut braid trim in half and glue diagonally across the outside corners bringing ends to the underside.

6. To finish inside of cover, fuse webbing to fabric lining section. Remove paper backing and fuse over cut edges on inside cover.

7. Insert note paper.

Covered Wastebasket or Perfect Plant Holder

Materials

- ½ yd decorator fabric
- Medium size plastic planter (10" diameter)
- ½"-wide paper-backed fusible webbing strip
- 2½ yds of self-adhesive shirring tape
- 1 yd of braided tassel fringe
- Hot-glue gun and glue

How-to

1. Cut fabric rectangle 12" x 38".

2. Press 1" to wrong side along the long edges. Press under ½" on one short end. Cut two pieces of shirring tape, 44" long. Position tape ½" from pressed edges with ends extending beyond the fabric. Pull out cords slightly from one end and tie together. Fuse in place.

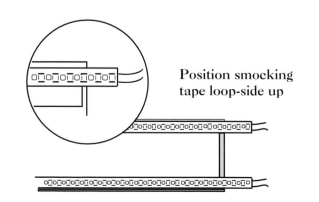

Position smocking tape loop-side up

3. Wrap fabric cover around planter, pulling up on the cords to shirr the fabric. Glue cut edge to one side of the planter. Adjust shirring to evenly distribute fabric around planter. Glue along upper and lower edges.

4. To finish, wrap braided fringe trim around the planter 2" from the upper edge and glue in place.

Tie long cord ends together in slip-knot and tuck all ends inside covering.

Desk Blotter

Materials

- Decorator fabric remnant
- 22" x 18" mat board
- 22" x 18" blotter paper
- ½"-wide fusible webbing strips
- Hot-glue gun and glue

How-to

1. Cut 2 – 7" x 22" fabric strips.

2. Press ½" to wrong side along all cut edges of strips. Fuse the long edges under with webbing strips.

3. Place fabric strips onto the upper and lower edges of the mat board and glue to the back of board along ends.

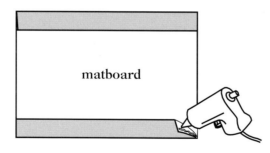

4. Tuck blotter paper into blotter under the fabric strips.

Bookmark

Materials

- Decorator fabric remnant
- Tassel
- Paper-backed fusible transfer web

How-to

1. Cut fabric 8" x 5". Fold in half lengthwise and cut across ends diagonally to form a point.

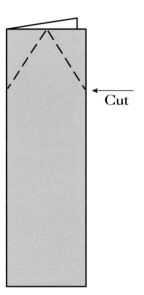

Cut

2. Unfold the fabric and press ½" to wrong side along all edges, cutting at the corners to eliminate bulk. Fuse transfer web to fabric over pressed edges. Peel off paper backing and fold in half lengthwise, sandwiching the tassel between layers at the point; fuse.

Chapter 6

Wonderful Window Wear

From animal-inspired to conversational prints, window wear is anything but boring. Custom design your window top treatments, such as valances, shades, and curtains, taking them from bland to grand.

Appliqued Kitchen Curtain

Iron-on tea cup transfers take only minutes to apply to ready-made sheers for a whimsical kitchen window treatment.

Materials

- Purchased sheer cafe curtains to fit your window
- Decorator fabric for appliqués (tea cup or other motifs)
- Paper-backed fusible transfer web
- $1\frac{1}{2}$"-wide gingham ribbon
- Air-soluble marker
- Ruler

How-to

1. Fuse transfer web to back of appliqué motif. Cut out design carefully from fabric, using a sharp pair of scissors.

2. Cut transfer web $1\frac{1}{2}$" wide and fuse to back of ribbon.

3. For the curtain, use a marker and ruler to draw a line 4" from and parallel to the hem. Mark the same on the valance, 2" from the hem. Remove paper backing from ribbon and place on curtain along marking. Fuse with a press cloth to avoid scorching sheer fabric.

4. Position tea cup appliqués along lower edge above ribbon, staggering motifs as desired. Fuse motifs in place with a press cloth.

Further embellish your curtain with fabric paint. Add dots of three-dimensional paint to decorate the cup. Or, paint whimsical swirls of steam rising from the cup.

Paint

Coach Shade

Create a colorful and relaxed window covering for a kitchen window. This one can be fused in a flash.

Materials

- Decorator fabric (A light-colored fabric will reflect sunlight and resist fading; medium-weight cotton, acrylic, or polyester has excellent sun resistance.)

- Lining fabric

- 1" and ⅝"-wide coordinating ribbon – the length of your window by 2 plus 12".

- $\frac{5}{8}$"-wide fusible webbing strips
- Mounting board – 1" by the window width.
- Angle irons and screws
- Staple gun and staples

How-to

1. Measure window width and length inside the frame. Cut fabric according to your measurements, adding 6" to the length for hems and 2" to the width for seam allowances. Cut lining fabric by your finished width and add 2" to the length measurement.

2. With right sides together, press under $\frac{1}{2}$" along the sides of the shade fabric. Then press under $1\frac{1}{2}$".

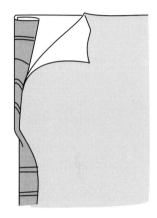

3. Place shade face down on a flat surface. Then, place wrong side of lining to wrong side of shade, having upper edges even. At the sides, place the lining under the hems. Insert strips of fusible web under side hems, and fuse.

4. Press $\frac{1}{2}$" to wrong side along the lower edge of the shade and lining. Fuse the hem in place. Fuse the opening closed at the upper edge with wrong sides together.

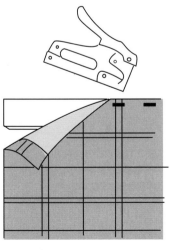

5. Staple top of shade to top of mounting board, aligning upper edge of shade to back edge of board.

6. Cut each ribbon into two equal pieces. Center the narrow ribbon over the wider and fuse in place. For ribbon placement, divide shade width by 4, or measure in from each end the desired placement distance and mark. Staple ends of ribbon to board at markings.

7. Attach angle irons to board. Mount shade inside the window frame. Pleat fabric at the lower edge and wrap ribbon from front to back around shade, making sure ribbon lengths are even. Staple end of ribbon to underside of board. To lower the shade, simply push the ribbons to the sides and allow shade to drop. Raise fabric by pleating it and replacing the ribbon.

Quick Tip

Cover mounting board with fabric by wrapping and stapling in place.

Reversible Tab Curtains, Two Looks in One

Double-faced curtains are a terrific way to get different looks at your window all year long. Made from three coordinatingfabrics, these banded tab-topped curtains slide on and off decorative rods for a quick change.

Materials

- Decorator fabric – 2 coordinating prints
- Coordinating fabric for bands and tabs
- Paper-backed fusible transfer web
- Pole set or decorative rod and finials to fit window
- 4 drapery weights
- Straight pins
- Needle and thread

How-to

1. Install pole or rod above your window.

2. Determine the finished length of the curtain by measuring from the bottom of the pole or rod to where you want the lower edge to fall. Subtract 2½" for the tabs. The width will be equal to two times the width of the pole.

3. Cut fabric panels (two fabric coordinates) according to your measurement. Note: You may need to fuse-seam fabric widths together to make panels, adding 1" for each seam. Cut side and lower bands 5" wide by the appropriate length plus 2". Cut two band sections for the upper edge 3" wide by the appropriate length plus 2". Cut tabs 5" x 7" (cut a total of 12 tabs for a 48"-wide window, or according to your window width.)

4. Fold tab pieces lengthwise, right sides together, and fuse-seam leaving short ends open. Turn right side out and press flat. Fold tabs in half crosswise and place on right side of curtain at the upper edge, placing cut ends even. Pin in place. Pin remaining tabs to curtain panels spacing them evenly apart.

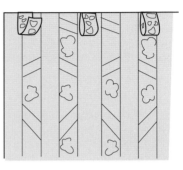

To secure tabs, hand or machine stitch them in place ½" from the edge. Flip tabs up and press seam allowance down.

5. Press ½" to wrong side along upper edge on remaining curtain section. With wrong sides together, place wrong side of curtain panels together matching upper pressed edges and lower cut edges. Pin in place.

6. Press ½" to wrong side along long edges of upper band sections. Cut transfer web 2" wide by the band length and fuse over pressed edges.

7. Remove paper backing from upper band sections and place over pressed edges on the curtain, on each side. Fuse in place. Cut bands even with panels at ends.

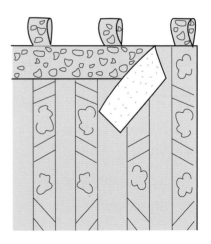

8. Press ½" to wrong side along lengthwise edges of remaining band sections. Cut transfer web 4" wide by the band length. Fuse over pressed edges. Allow to cool and remove backing. Wrap bands around cut edges of curtain panels to encase cut edges. Miter each corner (see General Techniques).

9. Tack drapery weights inside the bands at the lower corners. Fuse bands in place.

10. Slide pole through loops, and hang.

Quick Tip **Make a small window look larger by mounting the rod above the window molding, having it extend out beyond the window width.**

Angled Valance and Rod Pocket Curtains

This window treatment is basic but looks elegant when done in a variety of textured fabrics and topped with a simple valance.

Materials

- Sheer curtain fabric or lace
- Medium-weight decorator fabric for second curtain panel
- Decorator fabric and lining for valance
- Cording with a lip for valance – window width plus 10"
- Mounting board for valance – 4" x window width
- Angle irons
- ½"-wide fusible webbing strips
- Narrow curtain rod
- Yard stick
- Air-soluble marker
- Staple gun and staples

How-to (Curtain)

Note: These curtain panels do not have a header (the portion at the top of a rod-pocket curtain that forms a ruffle) since it is covered with the valance.

1. Determine the curtain length and add 3" for a rod pocket and 8" for a double-fold hem. Cut fabric the width two and one half times the finished window width. (Sheer fabrics can be three times the width of the rod for extra fullness.) Add 6" for side hems. (Sheer fabrics may have a finished lengthwise edge thus eliminating the need for side hems.)

2. Fuse-seam fabric widths for each panel, if needed.

3. Press 4" twice to the wrong side at the lower edge for a double-fold hem (see General Techniques). Fuse in place.

4. Press $1\frac{1}{2}$" to wrong side twice on the sides, and fuse.

5. Press $\frac{1}{2}$" to wrong side at the upper edge. Then press $2\frac{1}{2}$" for the rod pocket. Place fusible strip close to pressed edge; fuse. Insert rod through pocket, gathering fabric evenly. Hang over window. Tie back the sheer curtain, letting the decorator fabric hang straight down.

How-to (Valance)

1. Cut valance fabric and lining the width of the mounting board plus 10"
   for seam allowance, the returns, and some ease. To determine the cut
   length of the valance measure from where the board will be mounted to
   the desired finished length (usually ⅓ of the window length).

2. Cut valance to the appropriate width. To shape valance, place right
   side up on a flat surface. Then measure down one side to the desired
   finished length adding the seam allowance and 3" for the mounting
   board. Measure down 8" on opposite side. Using a yardstick and fabric
   marker, draw a diagonal line connecting two side markings. Cut valance and lining on marking.

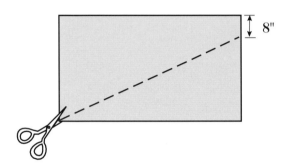

3. Apply fusible webbing strip to right side of cording lip.

4. Press ½" to wrong side along diagonal edge of valance. Fuse
   cording along pressed edge, turning ends under and
   applying liquid fabric glue to prevent raveling.

5. Fuse-seam lower and side edges of valance and
   lining, right sides together. Turn to right side and
   press. Finish upper edges by fusing wrong
   sides together.

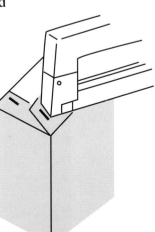

6. Press 3" to wrong side along upper edge and
   press returns at sides. Staple valance to top of
   mounting board, placing pressed fold along
   front edge of board. Miter corners around
   returns; staple in place to top of board.

7. Attach angle irons to board; mount on wall over
   curtain panels.

Show-off Roller Shade and Valance

Create a focal point in a room with this lavish floral appliqued roller shade and matching valance. It's really easy to do.

Materials

- Print fabric for valance and applique
- Solid, fade-resistant, medium-weight fabric for shade
- Foam-core board – width of window by 27" long (for a 40" wide window)
- Fusible backing (or purchase a shade kit*)
- Roller and hardware*
- ¾"-wide fusible webbing strip
- Paper-backed fusible transfer web

- Braid trim with tassels
- Tissue paper or newspaper for making valance pattern
- Masking tape
- Staple gun and staples
- Liquid fabric glue
- Velcro™ (hook-and-loop tape)

*Note: Shade making kits are available and come complete with fusible backing, roller and hardware.

How-to Shade

1. Install mounting brackets and roller according to manufacturer's instructions. Measure roller from inner edge of pulley to inner edge of end plug to determine finished width of shade. For length, measure from roller to sill.

2. Steam press fabric to remove any wrinkles and to pre-shrink. Cut fusible backing the width measurement and the length plus 10". Cut fabric according to width measurement plus 2" and length plus 12".

3. Center backing on fabric and fuse following manufacturer's instructions. Let cool.

4. Press under 1" on sides; fuse in place with webbing strip.

Quick Tip Instead of making side hems, carefully trim the fused shade cutting off 1" along the edges. Use a rotary cutter, mat board and ruler for a straight clean cut edge. If desired, use seam sealant along edges.

5. Press 2" to right side at the lower edge and fuse close to the cut edge to form a pocket.

6. Fuse transfer web to wrong side of print fabric for applique. Carefully cut around motif. Remove paper backing and position on shade. Fuse in place.

7. Using liquid fabric glue, attach braided tassel trim to lower edge so that the tassels hang just below the shade. Wrap ends under and glue. Insert hem stick in lower pocket.

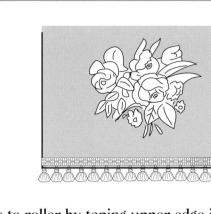

8. Attach shade to roller by taping upper edge in place. Check the direction of the roll. Some shades roll around the front and others to the back of the roller. Be sure shade is straight, then staple.

How-to (Valance)

1. Measure window width from outer edge of moldings. Measure down from top of molding to desired length. For a 40" wide or less, window valance is 27" long. Create a pattern by using the template (see Valance Template, page 124) provided for the swag and jabot. Trace on graph paper and enlarge it to fit your window measurements. Make a full-size pattern from tissue paper or newspaper and tape to window to check finished measurements.

2. Use pattern to cut foam-core board. Use same pattern to cut fabric, making sure to center floral motifs within the pattern. Cut fabric 4" larger around all edges of pattern.

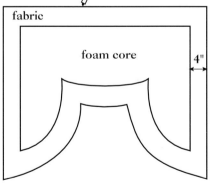

fabric

foam core

4"

3. Fuse transfer web to wrong side of fabric.

4. Position board on flat surface. Remove paper backing from fabric and place right side up on board. Fuse to board. Flip over and bring fabric ends to back side. Cut across corners to eliminate bulk. Fuse in place.

5. Separate Velcro™ strips and adhere it along the upper edge of valance back. Place the remaining strip along top edge of window molding. Mount valance to window adhering hook-and-loop strips together.

Roller Shade and Valance Options

Striped fabric is used to embellish a plain, store-bought fabric shade; or to make your shade from scratch, see previous pages for how-to's. Then coordinate a valance for a classically dressed window.

Materials

- ▌ Purchased shade
- ▌ Striped decorator fabric
- ▌ Lining fabric
- ▌ Mounting board – 4" x window width
- ▌ Paper-backed fusible transfer web
- ▌ Velcro™ (hook-and-loop tape)
- ▌ ¼" cable cord
- ▌ Staple gun and staple
- ▌ Liquid fabric glue
- ▌ Air-soluble marker
- ▌ Yardstick

How-to (Shade)

1. Mark placement lines for fabric trim on shade using marker and yardstick. Remove hemming stitch from shade and cut a gentle curve along the lower edge at each corner. Use a plate or other round object to mark. Cut along marking.

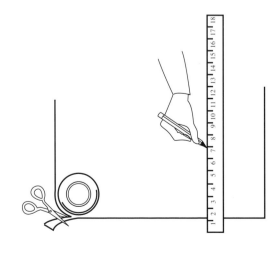

2. Fuse transfer web to striped fabric and cut. Remove backing and fuse to shade along markings.

3. To make self-covered piping, cut 2 bias strips of fabric 1½" wide by the shade width plus 2". Cut the same of transfer web. Fuse webbing to wrong side of bias strips. Remove backing and wrap strip around the cable cord so that the cut edges are even. Fuse edges together.

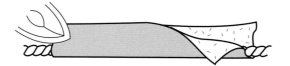

4. Fold up lower edge, clipping curve for a smooth finish. Secure with fusible web. Glue piping to lower edge. Make a pull from ribbon or cording by folding in half and gluing to the wrong side at the midpoint of the shade.

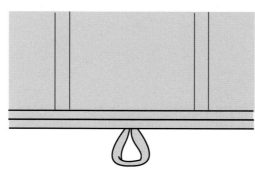

How-to (Valance)

1. Cut valance from decorator fabric by railroading it, cutting one continuous lengthwise piece rather than seaming widths of fabric together. Cut fabric and lining the width of the mounting board plus 10" for seam allowance, the returns, and some ease. To determine the cut length of the valance, measure from where the board will be mounted to the desired finished length (usually ⅓ of window).

2. Fuse-seam sides and lower edge, right sides together. Turn to right side and press. Finish upper edge by fusing wrong sides together.

3. Press 3" to wrong side along upper edge and press returns at sides. Staple valance to top of mounting board, placing pressed fold along front edge of board. Miter corners around returns; staple in place to top of board.

4. Attach angle irons to board; mount on wall over curtain panels.

Quick Tip

Make self-fabric welting by fusing narrow strips of fusible fleece to the wrong side of a bias strip. Fuse strips of webbing along lengthwise edge, fold and fuse ends together.

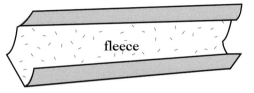

fleece

welting

Use iron-on loop and hook tape not only to hang decorative valances but also to hang bathroom vanity skirts, bassinet skirts, fabric-covered screens and balloons, and Roman or Austrian shades in no time at all. Iron-on loop tape comes with a compatible hook tape that is stapled or glued in place.

Tips for Decorator Sewing

• *Be sure to position print fabric motifs correctly. You'll need extra fabric; purchase an extra repeat for every fabric panel you need to cut.*

• *Cut all fabric panels in one direction for each project to guarantee that fabric motifs will be heading in the same direction.*

• *Use $\frac{1}{2}$" seam allowances when seaming is called for.*

• *When making window treatments, measure each window since all the windows in a room may not be the identical size.*

• *Make sure rods and mounting boards are installed on the level or curtains and valances will hang crooked.*

Chapter 7

Looking for simple and stylish ways to dress up your home? With just small amounts of fabric and some beautiful trims you can create wonderful accents for any room.

Pillows

Throw pillows are the simplest home furnishing items to create. They provide the finishing touch to a newly decorated room or perk up a tired one. Solid color pillows are lavishly trimmed with cords, bullions, gimps and fringes for a touch of opulence.

Tic-tac-toe Pillow

Blocks of fabric are fused together in a tic-tac-toe pattern and accented with flat braided trim.

Materials

- ¼ yd of 2 coordinating decorator fabrics
- 2 yds cording with a lip
- 2 yds flat braided trim
- 4 tassels
- 1 – 18" square pillow form
- Fusible interfacing
- Paper-backed fusible transfer web
- Liquid fabric glue
- Needle and thread
- Masking tape

How-to

1. Cut 4 – 6" squares from one fabric and 5 – 6" squares from coordinating fabric. Cut 1 – 18" square for pillow back. Cut an 18" square of fusible interfacing.

2. Place interfacing fusible side up, on a flat surface. Lay out pillow front sections, placing 6" squares in tic-tac-toe pattern (alternating coordinating fabrics), and butting the cut edges together. Fuse in place to interfacing.

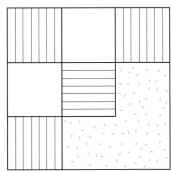

3. Glue braid trim over the cut edges of the pillow front.

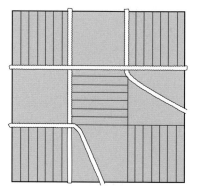

4. Fuse transfer web to right side of cording lip. Remove paper backing and fuse to outer edges of pillow front having lip even with cut edge. Clip into the cording lip at the corners. Where the cord ends meet, untwist the cord to separate. Tape each strand end to prevent raveling. Re-twist ends together and glue in place.

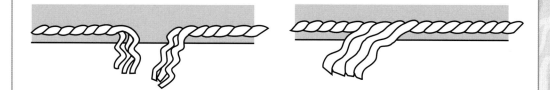

5. With right sides together, fuse pillow front and back around three sides. Clip across the corners to eliminate bulk.

6. Turn pillow right side out and press under ½" along opening. Insert pillow form and fuse or glue opening edges together. Note: The pillow cover is made slightly smaller than the pillow form for a plumper looking pillow.

Quick Tip Use clothespins to hold edges in place while glue dries.

7. Hand sew tassels at each corner.

Envelope Pillow

Materials

- ½ yd decorator fabric
- 1½ yds cording with a lip
- ¾ yd flat braid with tassels
- 1 – 12" square pillow form
- ½"-wide fusible webbing strips
- Liquid fabric glue

How-to

1. Cut 2 – 13" squares for pillow front and back.

2. Find the center front on one pillow square by measuring 6" down; mark with a pin. Glue tassel trim to front, beginning at one corner, taking it to the center pin and then up to the opposite corner.

3. With right sides together, fuse pillow front and back around three sides. Clip at the corners to eliminate bulk.

4. Turn pillow right side out and press under ½" along opening. Insert pillow form and fuse or glue edges together.

Satin Pillow Option

Materials

- ½ yd decoratore fabric
- 1 yd flat trim
- 1½ yds of 3"-wide fringe
- 1 – 12" square pillow form
- Liquid fabric glue
- ½"-wide fusible webbing strips

How-to

1. Cut 2 – 13" squares for pillow front and back.

2. Glue flat trim on the pillow front taking it from one edge to the opposite edge to form a triangular design.

3. Fuse 3" wide fringe to the pillow front, placing woven edge of fringe even with cut edge of pillow. Clip into the corner to ease the trim around.

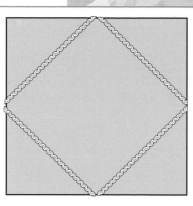

4. With right sides together, fuse pillow front and back around three sides. Clip across the corners to eliminate bulk.

5. Turn pillow right side out and press under ½" along opening. Insert pillow form and fuse or glue edges together.

Rectangle Satin Pillow

Materials

- ¾ yd satin fabric
- Coordinating print or textured fabric for insert
- 1 yd of 3"-wide fringe
- Flat braid trim
- Polyester fiberfill
- ½"-wide fusible webbing strips
- Liquid fabric glue

How-to

1. Cut front insert 8" x 12". Cut 2 side fronts 5" x 12". Cut 1 back 18" x 12".

2. Place side front sections on each long end of the front insert butting edges together. Glue flat braid trim over cut edges. Allow to dry.

3. Fuse fringe to pillow front at each short end, aligning cut edge of pillow with woven edge of fringe.

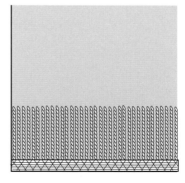

4. With right sides together, fuse pillow front and back around three sides. Clip at the corners to eliminate bulk.

5. Turn pillow right side out and press under ½" along opening. Stuff with fiberfill, and fuse, glue, or hand sew edges together.

Monogram Pillow

- Purchased pillow
- 1 yd cording without a lip
- Straight pins
- Hot-glue gun and glue

How-to

1. Knot ends of cord. If desired, use liquid glue or fabric sealant on ends to prevent raveling.

2. Arrange cord on pillow front to form desired letter and pin in place.

3. Glue cord to pillow.

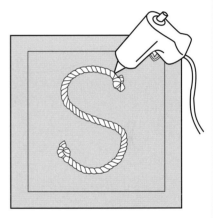

Tapestry Wall Hanging

Add old-world charm to any room with a tapestry wall hanging. Hang by decorative tabs on the wall with a brass rod and wrap with gold cording. Or this wall hanging can easily be made into a rug or throw by eliminating the tabs.

Materials

- 2 coordinating tapestry fabrics, one for the center section and one for bands and tabs
- 3 yds of thick cording without a lip
- Paper-backed fusible transfer web
- Fusible craft backing or a stiff interfacing
- Decorative rod and finials
- Liquid fabric glue

How To Make A Pillow Form

Make your own pillow forms in any size or shape. Use cotton or muslin fabric, cut 1" larger than finished size. Fuse-seam three sides, cutting at corners diagonally to eliminate bulk. Turn right side out and stuff with polyester fiberfill. Fuse, glue, or hand sew opening closed. Insert in pillow cover

- T-square
- Optional: 4 tassels, drapery weights

How-to

1. Determine desired size of finished wall hanging based on the tapestry design woven in the fabric. Straighten fabric using a T-square (see General Techniques) and cut.

2. Cut banding strips 5" wide by the appropriate length plus 2". Cut one band for the lower edge 5" by the width plus 2" finished. Cut two band sections for the upper edge 3" wide by the appropriate length plus 2". Cut tabs 5" x 7". (Cut a total of 8 tabs for a 48" wide hanging.) Cut fusible backing the same as the finished wall hanging.

3. Fuse interfacing to wrong side of wall hanging.

4. Fold tab pieces lengthwise, right sides together, and fuse-seam leaving the short ends open. Turn right side out and press flat. Fold tabs in half crosswise and place on right side of tapestry at the upper edge, placing cut ends even. Pin in place. Pin remaining tabs to front spacing them evenly apart.

To secure tabs, hand or machine stitch them in place ½" from the edge. Flip tabs up and press seam allowance down.

5. Press ½" to wrong side along long edges of upper band sections. Cut transfer web 2" wide by the band length and fuse over pressed edges.

6. Remove paper backing from upper band sections and place over pressed edges on each side of the wall hanging. Fuse in place.

7. Press ½" to wrong side along lengthwise edges of remaining band sections. Cut transfer web 4" wide to fit band length. Fuse over pressed edges. Allow to cool and remove paper backing. Wrap bands around wall hanging to encase cut edges. Miter the corners (see General Techniques). Fuse in place. Glue corners under miter to secure.

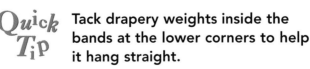

Quick Tip Tack drapery weights inside the bands at the lower corners to help it hang straight.

8. Slide pole through loops and hang. Knot ends of cording, placing a dab of glue at ends to prevent raveling. Wrap around pole at each end for accent.

Quick Tip Purchase four large tassels and glue to each end of the cording.

Throw

Casually draped on a chair or sofa, this fringed throw adds color and texture to any room setting. Make it square or rectangular and if desired, line it in coordinating fabric for versatility.

Materials

- 2½ yds of 54"-wide decorator fabric (preferably one that does not have a distinct right and wrong side)
- 6¾ yds of coordinating 6"-wide bullion fringe
- ⅝"-wide fusible webbing strips
- T-square
- Fabric sealant
- Liquid fabric glue

How-to

1. Straighten fabric using a T-square and cut a 54" square.

2. Press ½" to the fabric's right side along all edges. Fuse the bullion fringe over the pressed edges easing fringe header around each corner; then miter the trim header. Use glue to secure in place.

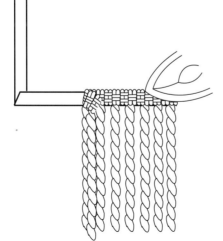

Apply fabric sealant at the cut end. Fold under the end and apply a small amount of liquid fabric glue.

Magazine Holder

Here's a convenient place to store your favorite magazines or books.

Materials

- Rectangular cardboard box (approximately 12" x 5" x 13" high)
- Decorator fabric
- Coordinating fabric for lining
- Paper-backed fusible transfer web
- Cording without a lip
- Cardboard insert cut to fit bottom of box
- Utility or mat knife
- Ruler
- Marker
- Hot-glue gun and glue

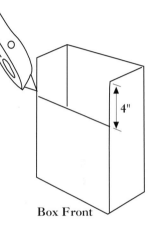

Box Front

How-to

1. Use mat knife to remove flaps from box.

2. Measure 4" down from the top and mark across the width of the box. Cut along marking.

3. Fuse transfer web to fabric. Do not remove paper-backing at this time.

4. Place fabric face down on flat surface. Lay box with cut side face down on paper backing. Wrap fabric around box, overlapping ends at the back edge. Mark cut outline on paper backing. Mark a second line 1" from first marking. Cut along second marking. Remove paper backing and fuse fabric to box, turning cut end under ½" at the center back. Glue in place. Bring ends around the bottom and miter the corners.

5. Cut fabric to fit box bottom. Press ½" to wrong side along each edge. Cut transfer web to fit and fuse over cut edges. Remove backing and place on bottom to cover cut edges. Fuse.

6. Fuse transfer web to lining. Remove backing and place lining inside box. Trim fabric around the opening leaving ½" to turn under. Turn ½" to wrong side along one center back edge. Fuse to box.

7. Make an insert to hold lining in place. Cover insert with fabric, and fuse. Place insert into bottom of box; insert should fit snugly.

8. Glue cording around opening edges to cover seams. Tuck ends of cord to inside and glue.

Footstool

Give your feet a break and rest them upon a fringed footstool.

Materials

- ▌ 3 – 6"-tall wooden legs (available at lumber stores)
- ▌ Mounting hardware for legs
- ▌ 12"-diameter plywood round
- ▌ 1 yd decorator fabric

- 1 – 14" round pillow form
- Fusible fleece batting
- 1½ yds of 6"-wide bullion fringe
- 1½ yds braid with tassel fringe
- Straight pins
- Hot-glue gun and glue
- Staple gun and staples

How-to

1. Attach mounting hardware and legs to plywood round.

2. Place pillow form on top of round and cover with batting. Lightly fuse batting to pillow. If desired, add a second layer of batting. Staple batting to plywood round along the outer edges and cut off excess.

Scout out second-hand furniture shops and flea markets for old footstools to cover.

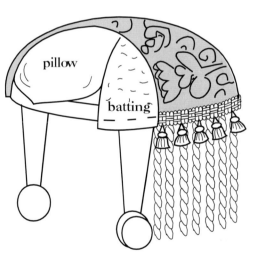

3. Lay fabric over top of batting and staple in place. Cut excess fabric even with lower edge of plywood.

4. Glue 6" bullion fringe on edge of plywood round over stapled fabric using pins to help hold fringe in place as you go. Glue tassel fringe over bullion fringe.

Tablecloth, Placemats, and Napkins

Make a stylish setting for a special meal or for everyday. Layer placemats over the tablecloth or use them on their own.

Tablecloth

Materials

- Decorator fabric (with no right or wrong side) for square or rectangular tablecloth
- Flat braid trim
- Paper backed fusible transfer web
- ½"-wide fusible webbing strips
- Liquid fabric glue

How-to

1. Measure length and width of tabletop, then determine drop (usually 10" – 12"). The finished size will be the width plus twice the drop length, and the length plus twice the drop length. Add 3" all around for hems.

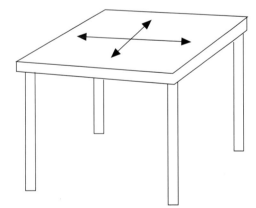

2. Cut fabric and fuse 3"-wide strips of transfer web on the right side along the edges of the cloth.

3. To hem, turn up 3" to the right side. Miter corners (see General Techniques) and fuse in place.

4. Using liquid glue, attach braid to cloth over the cut edge of the hem. Miter the corners of the braid.

5. If needed, dab glue into the mitered corners to secure.

Placemats

Materials

- 1½ yds of decorator fabric – 2 coordinating fabrics for 4 reversible 18" x 22" mats
- 8 yds flat braid
- 4 tassels
- ½"-wide fusible webbing strips
- Air-soluble marker
- Ruler

How-to

1. Cut 4 – 19" x 23" fabric rectangles. For each placemat, measure 14" at sides and mark. Mark center along end. To form a point, draw a diagonal line from the center marking to each side marking. Cut along marking.

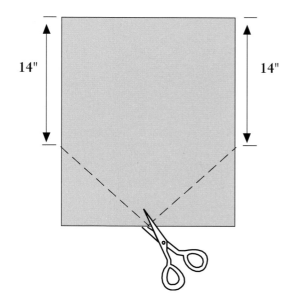

2. Fuse-seam sides and lower pointed edges of mats leaving the upper edge open. Cut diagonally at the corners to eliminate bulk. Turn right side out and press.

3. Turn ½" to wrong side at the upper edge and fuse closed.

4. Mark a rectangle on one side of the mat for the trim placement. Glue trim in place.

5. Hand sew or glue tassels to point.

Tassle

Napkins

Materials

▌ Decorator fabric – 15" square for each napkin

▌ ⅜"-wide ribbon in two coordinating colors

▌ Liquid fabric glue

▌ Twisted cord with tassels

How-to

1. Cut as many squares of fabric as needed for napkins.

2. Glue one ribbon along the cut edge of each napkin on the wrong side, looping the ribbon so it extends beyond the napkin at each corner.

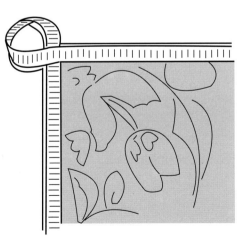

3. Glue a second ribbon to the right side of the napkin over the first, looping it at the corners and encasing the cut edges.

4. Wrap cording around napkins and tie to display.

Chapter 8

Gift Giving Ideas

Precious handmade gifts don't have to take hours to make. Use fusing techniques to easily and quickly create beautiful items that just look like they took time to create.

Sewing Basket

- ¾ yd of 54"-wide decorator fabric
- 2 ½ yds twisted cording without a lip
- ¾ yd twisted cording without a lip in a second color
- 1½ yds of tassel fringe
- ¾ yd of tassel fringe in a second color
- Fusible fleece batting
- Paper-backed fusible transfer web
- Cardboard or mat board
- Cookie tin or the like (8" tall and 7" diameter)
- Fabric glue
- Fabric sealant
- Hot-glue gun and glue
- Needle and thread

How-to

1. Cut fleece 10" x 26". Wrap outside of tin with fleece, having 2" extend beyond the upper edge. Glue with fabric glue.

2. Cut fabric 26" x 26" for the basket. Press ½" to wrong side along one edge. Wrap fabric around tin over the fleece, having 4" extending beyond lower edge, and the pressed side edge overlapping the cut edge along the basket side. Tuck the remaining fabric to the inside over the upper edge. Glue in place.

3. For the lid, trace a 13" diameter circle onto paper-backed fusible web and fuse to fabric. Cut circle and remove paper backing. Then cut 3 – 7" diameter circles from cardboard, 1 of fabric and 2 from fleece. Trace 3 – 7" circles onto paper-backed fusible web and fuse to remaining fabric. Cut along markings and remove paper backing. Fuse fabric to cardboard circles.

4. For the bottom, pull fabric slightly around the edge and pleat evenly. Glue using a hot glue gun. Place one cardboard circle over bottom to cover raw edges. Glue in place.

5. On inside, lap pressed edge over raw edge along the side and glue. Smooth out fabric, pleating at intervals or the bottom of the basket; then glue. Trim one cardboard circle slightly to fit inside snugly. Dab fabric glue on wrong side of cardboard insert and place into the bottom to cover the raw edges.

6. To make lid, glue fleece to one of the remaining cardboard circles having 1" wrap under to the inside and leaving an opening to stuff. Place a handful of batting under the fleece until it makes a smooth domed top. Glue opening closed.

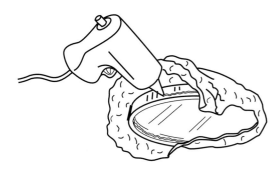

7. Thread a needle and make a long running stitch (see General Techniques) ½" from the edge of the lid fabric. Center fabric over batting, right side up and fuse lightly. Pull on the thread to gather the ends around the lid.

Wrap fabric around to the inside of the lid and distribute gathers evenly. Glue in place. Glue two fleece circles over raw edges on inside of lid. Fuse transfer web to remaining fabric circle and remove backing. Fuse over fleece. To finish inside, glue a narrow piece of twisted cording around the cut edge of the circle. Glue the wide twisted cording around the circumference of the lid. Apply fabric sealant or glue to cut ends of cord to prevent fraying.

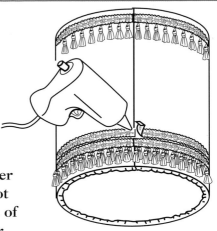

8. To embellish basket, wrap and pin the tassel fringe around the upper edge, turning under one end and lapping the other. Glue in place. Wrap the remaining fringe around the bottom of the basket so the tassels just come to the end. Lap the second color over the first and glue.

9. To make a carrying handle, braid together three pieces of 20" long twisted cord. Knot ends. Glue or hand sew the knotted ends of the cord to inside of basket 1" from upper edge at opposite sides.

Hat Pincushion

Materials

- Fabric remnant
- ½ yd lace edging
- ½ yd of ⅝"-wide ribbon
- Fusible interfacing
- Polyester fiberfill
- Paper-backed fusible transfer web
- Liquid fabric glue
- Needle and thread

How-to

1. Cut 3 – 8" diameter circles; 2 for the brim; 1 for the crown. Cut 1 – 8" diameter circle of interfacing.

2. Fuse interfacing to wrong side of one brim section. Fuse transfer web to the other.

3. Remove paper backing and fuse the brim sections wrong sides together. Glue lace edging over cut edges with liquid glue.

4. With a needle and thread, make a running stitch (see General Techniques) around the circumference of the crown. Pull up on thread to gather.

5. Stuff crown with fiberfill. Center crown on brim and attach using a hot-glue gun.

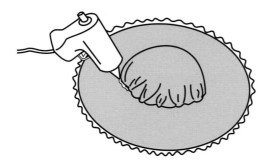

6. Wrap ribbon around base of crown and tie into a bow. Glue in place.

Ribbon-lattice Pincushion

This elegant pincushion can easily fill-in as a place to display hair pins, jewelry, and earrings.

Materials

- 2 – 12" fabric squares
- 1½ yds flat braid trim
- 1¾ yds of ½"-wide ribbon
- 4 small tassels
- Polyester fiberfill
- Straight pins
- Flat buttons
- ½"-wide fusible webbing strips
- Needle and thread
- Liquid fabric glue

How-to

1. Cut lengths of ribbon to run diagonally across the cushion front, allowing ½" extra at each end. Pin to fabric across opposite diagonals, keeping ribbons parallel to each other.

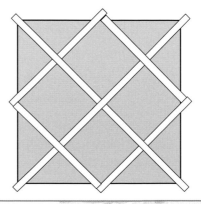

2. With a needle and thread, make small tacking stitches where the ribbons intersect to hold them in place.

3. With right sides together, fuse cushion front and back around three sides. Clip at the corners to eliminate bulk.

4. Turn right side out and press under ½" along opening. Stuff with fiberfill and fuse or glue edges together.

5. Glue braided trim around the outer edges.

6. Pin buttons through holes and attach to cushion at ribbon intersections.

Home Sweet Home Wall Hanging

A simple motif and crazy quilt border makes a delightful wall hanging. Precut letters have a fuzzy touch and are ready to peal and fuse.

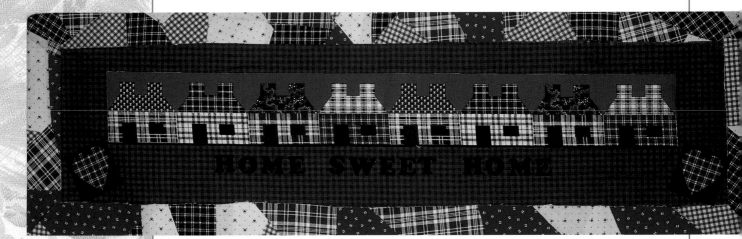

Materials

- Pre-printed fabric with large house motif
- ½ yd background fabric
- Remnants of four different coordinating print fabrics
- Muslin remnant for quilt foundation
- Fusible lettering
- Fusible fleece
- Paper-backed fusible transfer web
- Picture hangers

How-to

1. Cut 2 pieces of background fabric (1 is used for the background and 1 for the back) a suitable size for house motif; cut 1 of fusible fleece. Cut 2 strips of muslin for quilt borders 2" longer than the finished size (border width is 2" wide or wider depending on finished size of wall hanging).

2. Fuse transfer web to wrong side of fabric motif. Remove paper backing and center on the front of the background fabric; fuse. Fuse fleece to wrong side on front of background fabric. Fuse transfer web to backing fabric; then place over fleece and fuse.

3. To make crazy quilt border, fuse transfer web to wrong side of coordinating print fabrics. Cut odd shapes from fused fabric and arrange on muslin strip (foundation fabric). Vary the placement of the different sizes and shapes, alternating colors and prints, fitting them together like a puzzle.
   Be sure to overlap the edges slightly so that no foundation fabric is showing. Once you have achieved the desired look, cut lengthwise edges to straighten.

4. Fuse transfer web to wrong side of crazy quilt borders. Remove backing. Wrap borders around fleeced-backed wall hanging encasing all cut edges and lapping ends. Miter corners (See General Techniques) and fuse in place.

5. To hang crazy quilt wall hanging, attach picture hangers to the back at the upper corners.

Quilt Style Wall Hanging

Hung on a door or in an entryway, this wall decoration adds color and personality to any room. A three-dimensional effect is achieved when fusible fleece backs the fabric cutouts.

Materials

- Preprinted fabric for cutouts
- Background fabric
- Assorted buttons
- Fusible fleece batting
- Paper-backed fusible transfer web
- Liquid fabric glue
- Stick and twine for hanging

How-to

1. Fuse fleece to wrong side of fabric over preprinted motifs. Cut fleece-backed fabric around motif.

2. Cut fusible transfer web for each cutout and fuse over fleece. Remove paper backing and position cutouts on background fabric. Fuse in place.

3. Cut bands the desired width plus 1". Press ½" to wrong side along each edge. Cut transfer web to fit. Fuse webbing over pressed edges, allow to cool and remove paper-backing. Wrap bands around long edges of wall hanging and fuse in place.

4. Turn 3" to wrong side at the upper edge and fuse a strip of webbing close to cut edge (forming a casing). Fuse-hem the lower edge.

5. Decorate the wall hanging by fusing additional appliqué cutouts and gluing button clusters where desired.

6. Insert stick through casing and tie twine around each end. Hang from twine.

Fabric-Covered Photo Frames

Showcase your favorite pictures in frames that tell a story. Frames are easy and inexpensive to do and can be personalized in unique ways to suit the photo. (Also see picture frame shown in Chapter 5, The Desk Set.)

Fabric Frame

Materials

- ¼ yd fabric
- Heavy cardboard, mat board or precut mats for the frame front
- Fusible fleece
- Paper-backed fusible transfer web
- Pencil or fabric marker
- Ruler

- ▌ Mat knife
- ▌ Hot-glue gun and glue
- ▌ Optional: plastic insert to fit opening

easel

How-to

1. Determine desired size of frame and frame opening. Mark cardboard and cut (or use precut mat). Cut back ½" smaller than the front. Cut a cardboard rectangle, angling corners at the bottom for the frame easel.

2. Cut 2 fabric pieces for front and back and 1 fleece 1" larger than frame. Cut 1 fabric for the back facing and 1 for the easel. Fuse each of the fabric pieces with paper-backed web.

3. Fuse fleece to frame front. (For a more padded frame, cut two layers of fleece. Fuse the second layer on top of the first.)

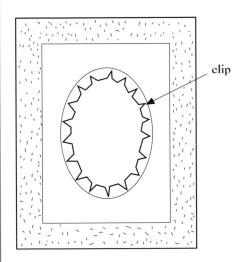

clip

4. Remove paper backing from one fabric and place fusible side down on center of frame over fleece. While holding frame in place, trace around the opening with a pencil or fabric marker. Draw a second line ¾" in from the first line. Cut opening along second line. Clip curves and into corners, stopping ⅛" from first marking.

5. Working alternately at opposite ends, turn ends to back of frame over mat cutting corners diagonally to reduce bulk; fuse. Turn and fuse other ends in the same way. Turn clipped edges to the back and fuse along frame opening. Be sure to pull gently and evenly as you fuse.

6. Remove paper backing from back section. Center mat board back on the fabric's wrong side. Cut at corners diagonally and miter; fuse. To cover back, remove paper backing from lining section and fuse to back (covering raw edges).

7. Cover easel with fusible fabric.

8. To assemble frame, place wrong wide of frame front together with the lining side of back. Using a thin bead of glue, glue along three sides of frame close to outer edges. Leave bottom edge open to insert photo.

How-to customize frames

- *Glue charms, buttons, ribbons, and lace, or fuse fabric appliques to outside of frame.*
- *Use wallpaper and fuse to a wooden frame to coordinate with a room.*
- *Wrap frame with thread, yarn or wire before gluing backing in place.*
- *Decorate with fabric paint.*

Weigh glued frame down with a heavy book. Allow to dry. Glue easel into place at the back.

9. Insert picture through bottom opening and insert plastic if desired.

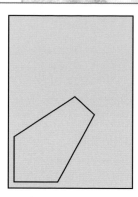

Quick Tip Look for frame kits at your local fabric and craft store. They come complete with precut cardboard pieces, fusible fleece and transfer web. You use your own fabric.

Covered Photo Album

Photo albums document family history. Make yours more personal by covering a plain album with novelty fabric and embellish it with trims and trinkets. Create a special place for wedding photos, baby pictures, school days, or vacation memories with custom covers that help tell a story.

Materials

- Purchased photo album
- Decorator fabric
- Fusible fleece batting
- Paper-backed fusible transfer web

How-to

1. Remove pages from album to cover. Open album and measure length and width. Cut fleece to fit. Add 4" to your length and width measurements and cut fabric and transfer web.

2. Place fleece, fusible side down, on cover and iron. Fuse transfer web to fabric. Remove paper backing and cover fleece on album; fuse. Wrap fabric around to the inside mitering the corners. At top and bottom of spiral binding, cut into the fabric easing it around the binding.

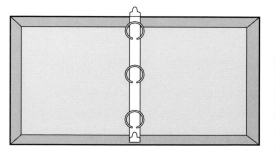

3. Cover inside front and back by fusing a piece of fabric over the cut edges.

Here's another way to personalize a photo album; before mounting a fabric-covered frame to a backing, glue it to the outside of the album for a special cover. Use iron-on transfers to decorate the album front or purchase precut designs that are ready to fuse.

Grandma's Brag Book

Special snapshots are ready for the showing. This handy roll-up wallet has clear vinyl pockets to display all your photos in style.

Materials

- 21" x 7" piece of decorator fabric
- ½"-wide double-fold bias tape
- Clear vinyl fabric
- Paper-backed fusible webbing strips (Double-stick adhesive strips designed for crafts can be repositioned and work best for this project.)
- 1 – ¾" button
- Ruler
- Fabric marker
- Press cloth

How-to

1. Round off the ends of the fabric rectangle. Cut vinyl fabric into 4 – 7" x 4" rectangles.

2. Place vinyl pieces horizontally along the fabric's wrong side, leaving ½" between them. Mark placement lines at lower edge of each. Remove vinyl sections.

3. Cut 4 – 7" long bias binding strips . Place an adhesive strip on the right side of the bias binding but only on one side. Remove paper backing and position along markings on fabric. Fuse in place.

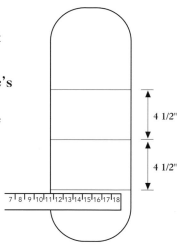

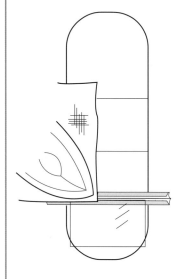

4. Open binding and place adhesive strip on half of the inside (the side not fused to the fabric). Remove paper backing. Place vinyl along adhesive, sandwiching it in the bias strip. Finger-press in place. Use a press cloth and the tip of your iron to adhere being careful not to iron on the vinyl.

5. Open remaining bias strip and place adhesive along both the inside edges. Remove paper backing from one half, beginning at the center on the top, and fold the bias tape over the fabric edge. When you come to the start, make a loop big enough to accommodate the button. Now, remove the paper backing from the remaining side and fuse in place with a press cloth using the tip of your iron, being careful not to touch the vinyl.

6. Starting at the end without the loop, fold the holder into a wallet shape. Stitch button in place and close.

Autumn Wreath

Turn over a new leaf and capture the beauty of Autumn's turning colors with a quilted wreath.

Materials

- ▌ ½ yd leaf print fabric (large print desirable)
- ▌ ½ yd backing fabric
- ▌ Fusible fleece batting
- ▌ Fusible webbing
- ▌ Dried yarrow in coordinating color

- Plastic decorative accent or bow
- 8" wire, macrame ring, or embroidery hoop
- Needle and thread
- Hot-glue gun and glue

How-to

1. Fuse fleece to wrong side of fabric.

2. Place webbing over fleece and layer wrong side of the backing fabric to webbing; fuse. You have created a sandwich consisting of decorator fabric, fleece, webbing, and backing fabric.

3. Using a sharp scissors, carefully cut around leaf motifs.

4. Quilt the leaves by hand sewing a running stitch or machine stitching along the veins of the leaves.

5. Arrange quilted leaves on wreath. Hot glue in place. Tuck in pieces of dried yarrow around the leaves and glue.

6. Glue decorative accent or bow to bottom of wreath, as desired.

GLOSSARY

Fusing and decorating terms used in the instructions.

Bar Tack: Reinforcing stitches worked over one another to secure an edge.

Batting: Lightweight polyester or cotton used for padding.

Bias cut: Diagonal grain of fabric.

Bias strip: Fabric strip cut on the bias; used for welting and ruffles.

Butt: Align two edges just so they meet without overlapping.

Cable Cord: White cord enclosed in fabric to make piping or welting.

Cording with a lip: Decorative cord that extends from a braided lip for insertion between two layers.

Drapery Weights: Small square, round, or chain weights to help the hang of a curtain.

Dowel: Wooden rod.

Ease: Extra fabric.

Fiberfill: Filling materials for pillows.

Finger-press: Flattening an area with your hand rather than an iron.

Finial: Decorative ends attached to a curtain rod.

Foam-core board: Lightweight cardboard-type material with foam center.

Grain: Lengthwise and crosswise weave of a fabric.

Header: Area of a curtain or valance that extends above a rod.

Hook-and-look-tape: Fastening tape with one rough hook side that attaches to a softer loop side.

Interfacing: Backing material fused on for extra stability.

Laminate: Waterproof plastic material fused to the right side of a fabric.

Meeting rails: Two horizontal pieces where the window sashes meet on a double-hung window.

Miter: 45° angle of a seam at a corner.

Motif: Design or patterns on a fabric.

Mounting board: Used to hold a window treatment mounted above the window.

Papier-mache: Made from paper and glue, and molded into lightweight boxes.

Pin mark: Straight pins used in fabric to indicate placement.

Railroading: Fabric cut horizontally rather than vertically.

Rod pocket: Casing used to hang a curtain.

Sandwich: Placing a third layer between two outside layers.

Seam sealant: Liquid applied to prevent raveling.

Self-fabric: Using same fabric as the main project (i.e. self-fabric piping).

Selvage: The finished lengthwise edges of a fabric.

Shirring tape: Band of fabric with cording woven in. When fused to a fabric and the cords are pulled, the fabric is gathered.

Squaring fabric: Straightening the ends of a fabric.

Trim: Fringes, braids, piping used to embellish an item.

Valance: Short treatment hung from the top of a window.

Show-off Roller Shade and Valance

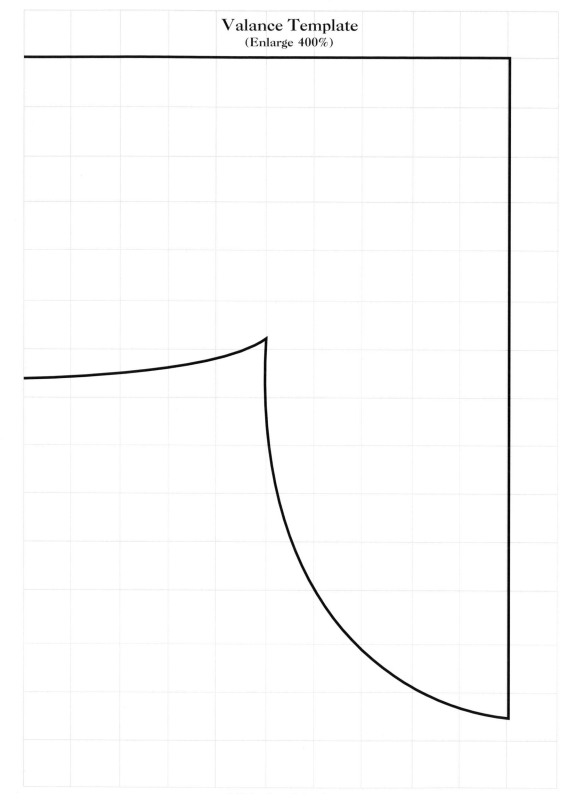

Valance Template
(Enlarge 400%)

(center)
Add or subtract width here.

1/2 inch = 2 inches

METRIC EQUIVALENTS

INCHES TO MILLIMETERS AND CENTIMETERS
MM—millimeters CM—centimeters

Inches	MM	CM	Inches	CM	Inches	CM
⅛	3	0.3	9	22.9	30	76.2
¼	6	0.6	10	25.4	31	78.7
⅜	10	1.0	11	27.9	32	81.3
½	13	1.3	12	30.5	33	83.8
⅝	16	1.6	13	33.0	34	86.4
¾	19	1.9	14	35.6	35	88.9
⅞	22	2.2	15	38.1	36	91.4
1	25	2.5	16	40.6	37	94.0
1¼	32	3.2	17	43.2	38	96.5
1½	38	3.8	18	45.7	39	99.1
1¾	44	4.4	19	48.3	40	101.6
2	51	5.1	20	50.8	41	104.1
2½	64	6.4	21	53.3	42	106.7
3	76	7.6	22	55.9	43	109.2
3½	89	8.9	23	58.4	44	111.8
4	102	10.2	24	61.0	45	114.3
4½	114	11.4	25	63.5	46	116.8
5	127	12.7	26	66.0	47	119.4
6	152	15.2	27	68.6	48	121.9
7	178	17.8	28	71.1	49	124.5
8	203	20.3	29	73.7	50	127.0

METRIC CONVERSION CHART

Yards	Inches	Meters
⅛	4.5	0.11
¼	9	0.23
⅜	13.5	0.34
½	18	0.46
⅝	22.5	0.57
¾	27	0.69
⅞	31.5	0.80
1	36	0.91
1⅛	40.5	1.03
1¼	45	1.14
1⅜	49.5	1.26
1½	54	1.37
1⅝	58.5	1.49
1¾	63	1.60
1⅞	67.5	1.71
2	72	1.83

Index

 **About the Author**

Karen is a magazine writer and book editor who specializes in fashion, sewing, home decorating, and crafts. Having been Corporate Education Manager for The McCall Pattern Company and an Educational Consultant for several sewing machine companies, she began free lancing in 1992. Since then her work has appeared in McCall's Pattern Magazine, Sew News, Family Circle, What's New In Home Economics, Sewing Decor and Vogue & Butterick's Home Decorating Projects book. Most recently she compiled and edited The Experts' Book of Sewing Tips and Techniques by Rodale.

Ms. Kunkel is the former host of "Karen's Craft Corner", which aired on an ABC affiliate network in Albany, NY twice monthly.

A graduate with a B.A. in Home Economics from Plattsburgh State University in New York, Karen has been fortunate to turn her hobby into a career.

ACKNOWLEDGMENTS

Fusible products courtesy of Conso® Products Co.; Coats & Clark; Dritz®;

HTC-Handler Textile Corporation; Freudenberg-Pellon™ products;

St. Louis Trimming; Therm O Web; What's New Ltd.

Window hardware courtesy of Interior Expressions™ by Dritz®.

Bathroom fabric courtesy of Concord House.

Trims courtesy of C. M. Offray & Sons, Inc.; Hollywood® Trims by Dritz®

Pressing Boards courtesy of june tailor.